to Jim Buchanan

complements of

Marshall Colberg

FACTORS IN THE LOCATION OF
FLORIDA INDUSTRY

FLORIDA STATE UNIVERSITY STUDIES

Number Thirty-six

FACTORS IN THE LOCATION OF FLORIDA INDUSTRY

by

M. L. Greenhut
and
Marshall R. Colberg

THE FLORIDA STATE UNIVERSITY
Tallahassee
1962

Printed and bound in the United States of America
by the E. O. Painter Printing Company, DeLand, Florida

Published under the Auspices

of

THE RESEARCH COUNCIL

The Florida State University

EDITORIAL COMMITTEE

Ruth Connor, *Chairman*

Werner A. Baum   Russell H. Johnsen

Homer A. Black   Raymond E. Schultz

Vincent V. Thursby

EDITOR

James A. Preu

CONTENTS

PREFACE

Surveys of industrial location are based usually on questionnaires which require check list answers. All too often, the terms employed in the questionnaire mean different things to different people, depending upon individual perspectives and backgrounds—a condition which reflects lack of a theoretical system to support the questionnaire. It is in this respect that our book is unique, for it presents a questionnaire survey based on, and framed by, economic theory. Each term used in the questionnaire has a specific meaning, as given to it in turn by the theoretical system which supports the survey.

One may, of course, ask how respondents can be advised of our "theory" and hence accept and use the words in the questionnaire as we desired. Our answer to this query will be found in several places later on. For the moment, suffice it to say that we believe we have approached, if not fully attained, this end. Most significantly, it would then follow that the present book does not provide a mass of statistical data useable by development commissions for the simple end of claiming locational accomplishments. Rather, it provides statistical information which lends itself to analysis so that the factors underscoring the economic development of a region or state may be determined.

We suggest that readers of this volume and those who work with the statistics included herein will be able to rely on the facts that: (1) the respondents who checked a given term, phrase or expression, such as "access to markets," had the same general idea about the meaning of the particular expression, (2) the designated factor (*i.e.,* term, phrase, or expression) is itself identifiable as part of a theoretic system so that its place within a complete body of thought can be appreciated by the reader, and (3) the permutations and combinations that are possible when one uses a modern computer—some of which permutations and combinations are included herein—will reveal many industry characteristics, regional or area trends, and general location features of interest to those concerned with plant location and the economic development of a state or region.

One final preliminary is in order. We do not attempt herein an encyclopedic listing of information gained nor do we approximate a detailed explanation, or even a full description, of Florida's recent economic development. Our prime objective is simply to adapt location theory to the demands that empiricists place on it. In fulfilling this goal, we shall include a set of selected findings (*i.e.*, combinations) to provide a special picture of Florida's recent economic development, to suggest future trends, and to demonstrate the analytic potentials of location surveys. These special ends underscore the basic objective of this book.

The survey on which much of the book is based was made possible by a contract with the Florida Development Commission. Permission to publish the results privately was included in the contract and is gratefully acknowledged by the authors. The co-operation of officials at the Florida Development Commission was most helpful. Among these Mr. William Shelton, Mr. Richard Colley and Mr. George Hack contributed much by way of suggestions, criticisms, and editorial comments. A great many businessmen in Florida were, of course, basic contributors to the success of the location survey and many gave generously of their time in personal interviews as well as in filling out questionnaires.

The authors wish to acknowledge their thanks to Warren Pillsbury, Clinton Whitehurst, Samuel Skogstad, Joseph DiBerardino, Professor Levern Graves, and Professor Royal Mattice for their assistance in a research project which provided much of the material included in this book. Mrs. Gennelle Jordan, Jean Profitt, James Clark, and Lucy Jacoway have been most helpful in many different ways. Final expressions of debt are due and hereby extended to the Florida State University Research Council and the Inter-University Committee for Economic Research on the South for grants which enabled further study and provided final impetus to this book.

Tallahassee, Florida   M. Logan Greenhut
June 1, 1962   Marshall R. Colberg

CHAPTER I

INTRODUCTION

This book presents an analysis of Florida's recent industrial development. Many readers will conclude that it is a rather unconventional presentation, since we do not include statistics on per capita income, growth of state revenues and expenditures, employment, population characteristics and projections, and similar data. It is our view that this kind of information is well reported and readily available to all. What we attempt to do here is to *explain* rather than *describe* what has been happening in the area of industrial development. Like any explanation of economic events this will be an incomplete one, but it is hoped that most of the key factors, and some of the subsidiary factors, will be made evident.

The basic statistical reference source that we use is the findings of a study conducted by the authors of this book for the Florida Development Commission a few years ago. This statistical study of new industrial locations in Florida will serve as the principal source of data to be utilized. While the results should be of special interest to businessmen, local officials, and state officials in Florida, they also have a broader significance. Problems of attracting new industry differ somewhat from state to state and region to region. Yet there are many elements in common. It is hoped, therefore, that both the theoretical and statistical approach and the results of this study will be of utility outside of Florida as well as within the State.

Plan of Book

Chapter II describes the method used to distinguish the principal locational factors in the survey made for the Florida Development Commission. Chapters III and IV, respectively, describe in some detail the theoretical system and the statistical techniques used in that survey. Chapter V records some of our main findings as to why new manufacturing plants located in Florida in 1956 and 1957.

Chapter VI focuses attention on the problem of county development in Florida. It shows the largely dissimilar factors which induced location in the "urban" or "developed" counties compared with those which brought plants to the "rural" or "underdeveloped" counties in 1956 and 1957. Chapter VII describes some subsequent related events.

General Observations on the Location Survey

As was noted above, Chapters III and IV explain the theoretical and statistical bases for the survey of locational factors. Let us observe here why such explanations are required.

The validity of any survey depends upon the sampling technique, the response rate, the willingness and ability of the respondent to report truthfully and competently his practices, the capacity of the questionnaire to uncover the needed information, and the ability of the analyst to classify the replies in a meaningful way. These last two requirements (adequate questionnaire and meaningful classification) are actually rooted in the same base, namely, the theoretical system that underlies the survey. In the absence of an integrated system of thought to support a survey, one may acquire only the thought processes of particular individuals. And these thought processes may differ from one person to another *only* in the sense that terminologies may differ; nonetheless, seemingly different forces will appear statistically.

It is only when responses are elicited and interpreted in a systematic way that these responses (if sufficient in number and truthfully proffered) will have meaningful quantity. Those who read Chapter III will find recorded there the theory that supported this survey. They will note the basis which governed the classification given to answers. But for those who want to omit this reading, preferring to rely completely on the ability of the reporters of this project to have a workable and consistent pattern, we submit in Chapter II a brief classification and explanation of the factors into which the location process was divided. We add, however, the qualification that this forthcoming brief description can, at best, only gloss over the surface of possibilities that exist without showing the full significance and implications of the classification which supported the study.[1]

---

[1]Consider the statistic that 71 firms in the Fabricated Metals Industry located in Florida primarily to secure access to markets. (This is shown in Chapter V.) Just what is meant by this? What if Florida is the only market for the firm? What if the plant is the first of its kind for the firm? What if the firm has an older plant elsewhere in the country so that the Florida plant is, in fact, a

Chapter IV, as observed previously, goes into the statistical practices that were followed. Readers who are interested chiefly in derived data rather than in how the data were compiled may omit Chapter IV without loss of understanding or continuity.

One last thought in introduction must be noted and stressed. The location study on which the book is based centers attention upon the site-selection of new plants—a location analysis and survey which differs sharply from what would be designed to record the location factors claimed to be relevant by long established plants. In the new plant category, we find some fly-by-night concerns which located to take advantage of a "quick-deal"; we find also some concerns that are designed for permanancy but which unfortunately are poorly located; we find finally some concerns located in the belief that compliance with certain forces is necessary but which in time will experience a change in this belief. One might say that a study of new plant locations is then a study of site-selection factors while a study of long established locations is an investigation of plant location factors. But word distinctions such as these are not of great importance. What matters really is that we appreciate the existence of differences of this kind; otherwise, many of the findings recorded here can be misinterpreted.

The present volume stresses *new* plant locations for three reasons. First, the recent industrialization of Florida has been so rapid that empiric references to it are needed just to keep abreast of recent events and to anticipate, if possible, certain future events. Second, any survey of new plant locations helps to uncover some basic advantages that tend generally to have long lasting influence. *And,* to the extent that some cases are included in the survey which

---

branch plant location? What if the firm considered alternative markets before selecting Florida for the location of its plant; what if it did not? If, rather than accept the obvious cliché that access to markets must mean a strong market, we recognize that sufficient demand is a fundamental requisite for all economic activity, it becomes clear that not only respondents to a questionnaire but readers of the findings of a survey must have a clear idea about the meaning of the words which serve as the base for the statistic. If statistical accumulations and tabulations are to be significant, the definitions of variables by respondents to a questionnaire must be consistent. Yet remember that each respondent will have a different perspective (*e.g.,* a first plant location, a branch plant location, etc.). It follows that establishing reference points which carry common meaning to all firms regardless of industry type, firm type, and situation type becomes the key to effective economic research of the present kind. Failure to satisfy this need is equivalent to causing unlike things to be added.

the passage of time will show to have reflected improperly formed locations, there is the offsetting condition that some of the new plant locations will uncover completely new places and fields of opportunity, the potential of which would be obscured by emphasis on long established plants. Third, and most important, all business ventures are based on anticipation of things to come. A study of new plant locations uncovers these anticipations. It is oriented more to the future than is perhaps any other kind of industrial location study.

CHAPTER II

THE CLASSIFICATION OF FACTORS

The theory of location of an industrial plant can be viewed most simply as a part of the general theory of profit maximization usually employed to explain behavior of the firm. Managerial economics emphasizes rational behavior in such matters as price and output determination, employment, and capital budgeting but usually does not enter deeply into the problem of locating a plant in such a way as to obtain the most profitable relationship between demand and cost. A special problem involved in the location decision, both in theory and in practice, is that both demand and cost functions are dependent on location. Few key variables can reasonably be placed in *ceteris paribus*.

Modern organization theory emphasizes that "satisfactory" rather than "optimum" solutions are a common goal of business organizations. In theory, finding an optimum location requires that there be a thorough "search" in which the added cost of investigation is carefully balanced against the value of uncovering better sites. Large companies often treat the problem of location in much this way; smaller ones are likely to depend more on limited investigation and general experience of executives.

Whether or not search for an optimum location is carried out fully, nonpecuniary advantages and disadvantages can modify attitudes of locators. The *total* advantage of a location, pecuniary and non-pecuniary, should guide a locational decision. This is more true of a small enterprise, however, where the effect of non-pecuniary factors on one or a few executives who are closely and permanently tied to the firm should properly be given substantial weight. On the other hand, a branch plant of a large firm is apt to be located primarily with an eye to maximizing monetary profits of the firm as a whole. In an uncertain world, however, it should be recognized that profit expectations are unlikely to be single-valued. Consequently the attitude of company officials — their desire to be conservative or to gamble — is a subjective factor which is likely to enter into an otherwise objective analysis of profit potential at various locations.

For the purposes of our survey the factors of location were divided into three main classes: the demand factors, the cost factors, and the purely personal considerations. The demand factors include items A.1 and A.2 on the questionnaire (see end of this chapter). The cost factors include all of the B, C, D, E items and F.1 and F.2. The purely personal factor is item F.3.

The Personal Factor

The personal factor caused the greatest confusion among the businessmen respondents to our questionnaire. This confusion reflected the fact that oftentimes a person will locate a business in Florida because he wants to live in Florida but will select as his enterprise or venture a business that fits the area. *From his standpoint,* the personal factor determined the plant location; *from the business standpoint,* however, some other force (*e.g.,* a demand or cost advantage) makes the venture economic. For the purposes of our study, we had to distinguish the person from the business *whenever* the respondent contended that economic advantages exist in Florida in his line of activity. Under the distinction, we reserved the purely personal factor for uneconomic locations, that is, where, by claim of the respondent, he located a business in Florida even though he knew that if it were located elsewhere he would beyond all doubt secure greater monetary profits. Because we expected many respondents to have a different view of this factor than that which we hoped our general instructions would suggest, our group of analysts made follow-up contacts in each case of this kind to verify the respondent's questionnaire.[1]

The Cost Factor

The cost factor probably involved the least difficulty for the respondents. Only in special cases did our analysts note contradictions or possible contradictions in the reporting of cost advantages which required a follow-up inquiry and cross-checking with the respondents. Whatever difficulties did exist with respect to the

---

[1]Note that the questionnaire lists three closely related items which imply personal gratifications in the location process: (1) climate as it affects operations (item D.5), (2) climate as an attraction to top management (item F.1), and (3) the personal factor with economic advantage (item F.2). But while each of these implies personal gratifications in the plant location, they also involve an economic cost advantage. Accordingly, they are distinguishable from the personal factor that lacks economic basis, lying on an entirely different level from that one (item F.3).

elements making up costs will be evident during the discussion of certain aspects of the demand factor.

The Demand Factor

The demand factors of location, like the purely personal factor, involve certain complications that oftentimes required a double checking with respondents. For purposes of this report, *access to markets* (demand factor A.1) and *anticipation of growth of markets* (demand factor A.2) *indicated the general condition where the Florida market (existing or potential) was so attractive that even if costs were unfavorable in Florida, as distinct from costs in other market areas, the plant would have been located in this State. Ipso facto,* if costs were so favorable here that even if the Florida market were inferior to an alternative market the location would have taken place in this State, the Florida location is cost-determined. If both market and costs are favorable here, the factor of greater advantage serves as the primary cause of the location in Florida.

The Economic Factors Compared

Our concept of market required respondents to evaluate their location in the light of the next best alternative market area whenever an alternative was considered. Without this conception, we find (as explained in Chapter III) that one respondent might argue that markets brought him to Florida, whereas another respondent subject to comparable forces might claim that cost advantages caused him to locate in Florida. Clearly, when an owner or manager of a plant asserts that his plant is located efficiently, he is contending that he is selling a sufficiently large amount of goods at a low enough cost. Comparatively, if located elsewhere, he could not sell this same amount of goods at that same low cost. At best, he might sell a smaller amount at that cost or a larger amount at much higher costs.

Depending upon the person, a respondent might say that it is his sales (demand factor) that prompted his location or he may think of his advantage as a cost advantage. Under our classification and related instructions, all respondents should distinguish the market determinant from the cost factor in the same way. In the several cases where doubt developed concerning the respondent's compliance with the classification, our analysts made further inquiry by letter, phone call, or interview. Whether intuitive reaction causes replies to comply with instructions or whether careful thought supported the filling out of questionnaires is subject to dispute. But this much is true: the cases of doubt which led to follow-ups consistently verified the respondent's answers.[2]

Access to Florida Market

The focus of our study on Florida involved another complication that should be understood by all, including those who are not interested in the theoretic details of Chapter III. This complication ties up with the matter of definitions. Suppose, for example, that a firm wants to sell to a market in South Carolina and that it actually locates in Florida because the cost level that prevails in this State enables the company to sell in the South Carolina market at a lower delivered cost than would be possible if it located in South Carolina. Suppose further that the firm could have been located in Utah to sell in the Idaho market at a lower delivered cost level than is offered in the South but that the South Carolina market is much stronger than the Idaho market. In this case, we would find that it is really the South Carolina market that is the attractive force. But, for the purposes of our survey, we do not regard access to markets as the factor explaining the Florida location; rather, it is the cost factor which produced the advantage in Florida over, shall we say, any other southeastern state, and which factor therefore accounts for the location. Access to markets then means, in this report, access to the Florida market. In effect, that which sometimes appears as a cost determinant of location on the basis of a report issued to a state government would appear as a market-determined location factor in a survey that is being conducted under national sponsorship. Significantly, and fortunately, it is suggested that in the usual instance the meaning which most people would ordinarily attach to the words "access to markets" (*i.e.*, access to the Florida market) will coincide with the statistical references that we make to it.

The Statistical Tables

As a final preliminary note, it should be stated that in Chapters

---

[2]One interviewee in particular objected strongly to our classification. He stated that he understands "right well what we were doing but he was darned if he saw the reasons for our distinctions." Nonetheless, he had filled out his questionnaire perfectly.

V and VI we record many more statistics than can adequately be described in a book limited by time and space. Thus our descriptions will be selective and hence will be much more restricted than are the data recorded in the tables. Clearly, what interests one reader may extend beyond or may lie in different directions from those which interest other readers, or for that matter the present writers. Because the readers of this book will conceivably come from many different walks of life, because its uses will therefore vary from one person to another, we advise and suggest at this time that our descriptions should serve primarily as a general introduction to the finding of the survey. We believe that many special applications can be made of them by the various readers.

An important basis for classifying statistical results will be the stage of county industrial development as indicated by the Florida Development Commission. For the years 1956-57 a total of 48 counties were classified as "underdeveloped" while 19 were called "developed." The former are also commonly designated as "rural" and the latter as "urban." For the most part the counties considered to be underdeveloped have a lower per capita income than the other group. An interesting exception, however, is Hendry County which in 1959 had the highest per capita personal income but carried the "under-developed" designation.[3]

In Northern Florida 29 of the 34 counties were considered "underdeveloped"; in Central Florida 13 out of 20 were so classified; while in Southern Florida the developed counties outnumber the others 7 to 6.

---

[3]*Statistics of Personal Income, Population, Construction, Businesses, and Manufacturing for Florida Counties,* Bureau of Economic and Business Research, University of Florida, June, 1961, p. 3.

Survey Conducted by

DEPARTMENT OF ECONOMICS, FLORIDA STATE UNIVERSITY

For Florida Development Commission

FLORIDA PLANT LOCATION SURVEY

Part I — Company and Products

1. Name of firm _____
2. Address of plant _____
3. County _____ SIC Group _____ Code _____
4. Number of employees of plant: Present _____ Planned _____
5. Type of plant: (check one) ____ New firm or original main plant; ____ New branch plant; ____ Relocation of out-of-state plant. ____ Relocation of in-state plant.
6. In what State was the administrative office located before this plant was built? _____
7. Principal market area of new plant: _____ Florida; _____ Southeast; _____ National or other.
   If you checked Southeast please list principal States. _____
8. Is Latin America expected to be an important market (10% or more of total)?
   ____ Yes ____ No.
9. Products: _____

10. Use class of principal product: ____ for household use without further processing; ____ for household use after further processing; ____ for industrial use; ____ for construction use; ____ other.
11. Where do you obtain your principal raw materials and components?
    Raw Material — Component   Sources (city or state)
    1. _____   _____
    2. _____   _____
    3. _____   _____
12. Please list the subcontracting facilities that your firm uses.
    Type   Name and Address
    _____

Part II — Location Factors in the Industry

1. The major item of cost in an industry may not be an important locational factor. What matters is the differences in the cost item at alternative locations. Similarly, access to markets, though a vital consideration in any business, is an important "factor of location" only if the sales potential varies significantly at alternative locations. Please rank the four factors which typically are the most important in your industry. These need not be the same ones that dominated your own locational decision. (In Part III you will be asked to rank the three most important factors in your own decision.)

(1) _____   (3) _____
(2) _____   (4) _____

2. Is there any factor of location that is unique to your industry (example, special transport facilities) which you did not mention in the previous question because there are many alternative places offering this factor in an equivalent way?

_____
_____
_____

Part III — The Factors That Influenced Your Plant Location

1. How did you first become aware of Florida as a possible location for your operation?
   ( ) Florida Development Commission Advertising   ( ) Vacation trip to State
   ( ) Through business contacts in State   ( ) Chamber of Commerce contacts
   ( ) Others _____   _____

(Over)

2. Explanation of check list — The plant is located at a given place because this location is expected to yield greatest profits or satisfactions to the owner. Location in Florida may suggest that access to markets is so favorable that even though (or if) cost is higher than at other places the sales potential is sufficiently large to induce the location. Or, it may be that the market is about the same as at other locations, while certain cost savings indicate greater profits and thereby explain the location. Or some combination of these forces may, in fact, prevail. Indeed, personal satisfactions alone may have dominated, with economic values being sacrificed. Below are listed by category some important factors of location. Please check those which were considered to be important in guiding your company to its new Florida location. Later on you will be asked to rank these factors according to their importance.

A. DEMAND
1. ( ) Access to markets
2. ( ) Anticipation of growth of markets

B. LABOR
1. ( ) Amicable labor relations
2. ( ) Lower wages
3. ( ) Higher productivity
4. ( ) Florida labor laws
5. ( ) Availability of labor already in Florida
6. ( ) Ease of attracting out-of-State skilled labor (including research personnel)

C. RAW MATERIALS, COMPONENTS, FUEL AND ENERGY
1. ( ) Low seller's mill price on your raw materials and components
2. ( ) Low freight cost on obtaining raw materials and components
3. ( ) Availability of raw materials (Apart from price and freight cost)
4. ( ) Low cost of fuel
5. ( ) Low cost of electric power
6. ( ) Adequate supply and satisfactory type of water

D. OTHER PROCESSING COST CONSIDERATIONS
1. ( ) Low cost of capital
2. ( ) Availability of capital (Ease of borrowing)
3. ( ) Low freight cost on shipping final product
4. ( ) Adequate waste disposal possibilities
5. ( ) Climate (as it affects operations)

E. STATE AND COMMUNITY FACTORS
1. ( ) Community facilities (educational, medical, police and fire)
2. ( ) Community attitudes and aid
3. ( ) State and/or municipal tax structure
4. ( ) Aid from the Florida Development Commission

F. PERSONAL FACTORS
1. ( ) Climate (as an attraction to top management)
2. ( ) Personal (with economic advantages, e. g., friendship with customers, suppliers, or bankers)
3. ( ) Personal (without economic advantage)

G. FACTORS NOT LISTED
1. ( )
2. ( )
3. ( )

3. Please rank the three factors among those which you have checked that were most influential in causing you to choose a Florida location. These need not be the same as those which usually control in your industry. For example, "A" may typically be a more important factor than "B" and "C", but in selecting your location you may have sacrificed some advantages in "A" to gain the "B" and "C" advantages, etc.

1. _____ 2. _____ 3. _____

4. What factor or factors caused you to select the city in which you are located? Please rank if more than one factor was vital. _____

5. What main alternative location(s) in Florida did you consider? _____

What was its main advantage? _____
What was its greatest shortcoming? _____

6. What factors, if any, have you found to be unsatisfactory? _____

7. What factors, if any, were unsatisfactory, but were rectified by local interests? Please explain. _____

8. What factor or factors, if any, were most influential in causing you to consider locating in the South? Please rank if more than one factor was vital. _____

9. What main alternative location outside of Florida did you consider? _____

Name, Address and Position of Person Completing Questionnaire _____

(Date)

_____
(Name)

_____
(Address)

_____
(Position or Title)

Please return to:
Department of Economics
Florida State University
Tallahassee, Florida

CHAPTER III

THE THEORETICAL FRAMEWORK[1]

It is scarcely possible to overstress the need for common terminology in theoretical or empirical studies. The terminological problem in the field of location economics is illustrated by the following hypothetical examples.

Company A chooses for its plant a site in central Florida. The owners of the company contend that they gain many advantages at their location. Principal among these are savings in labor cost and taxes, which according to company officials enable them to sell to the New York market at a lower delivered price than is possible at any other location. When asked to select between access to markets on the one hand and lower labor costs and taxes on the other, they readily choose the latter combination as the main factor of location, *i.e.*, lower labor costs and taxes.

Company B chooses for its plant a site in central Florida. The owners of the company contend that they gain many advantages at their location. Principal among these are savings in labor cost and taxes, which according to company officials enable them to sell to the Georgia and South Carolina market at a lower delivered price than is possible at any other location. When asked to select between access to markets on the one hand and lower labor costs and taxes on the other, they hesitate perceptibly and somewhat uncertainly select the latter combination as the governing force, *i.e.*, lower labor costs and taxes.

Company C chooses for its plant a site in central Florida. The owners of the company contend that they gain many advantages at their location. Principal among these are savings in labor cost and taxes, which according to company officials enable them to sell to the central Florida market at a lower delivered price than is possible at any other location. When asked to select between access to markets and lower labor costs and taxes, they hesitate, argue, and eventually disagree. One claims that the lower costs describe

---

[1]In forming the present chapter, the writers have drawn heavily upon some material presented to the Florida Development Commission in their report "Why Industry Locates in Florida," and a paper by M. Greenhut, "Size of Markets Versus Transport Costs in Industrial Location Surveys and Theory," *Journal of Industrial Economics,* VIII (1960), pp. 172-184.

the main influence behind their location in Florida; the other contends that their site-selection provides them with access to markets. Eventually, they select the latter as their factor of location.

One may certainly ask whether the answers given by the spokesman for Company A, B, and C should be different just because the final product has to be shipped two, twenty, or one hundred miles rather than x, y or z miles? Assuredly from a national viewpoint, the cases would seem to be identical regardless of the location of the market.

Before any statistics can be presented which explain the factors of location in any area or state, and before a theoretical explanation of location forces can be offered, the basis for classifying and systematizing data must be explained. Unpopular as definitions may be, one cannot learn the reasons "Why Florida is Developing" without knowing what is meant by the phrases and words "access to markets," or location due to "labor costs," "raw material costs," "raw material availability," "personal considerations," and their like. For the present, we need concern ourselves only with the two main categories of location factors: demand and cost. We suggest first that the reader examine casually Part III of the questionnaire, which is reprinted at the end of Chapter II. In this connection, note that the demand factor, item A, includes access to markets and anticipation of growth of markets; the cost factor, which we will discuss and develop at length throughout this volume, includes items B,C,D,E, and elements of item F. A final main factor, purely personal considerations, need not be discussed at this time but will be explained in detail later in the chapter.

Some Definitions Relating to Demand and Cost

Every firm must have a market for its goods and services. Consequently, the vital requirement in every location decision is that the enterprise have some access to a market. Any survey of plant location could then take access to markets as *the* governing factor. In turn, the study would involve only a search for the subsidiary factors that affect location.

By assuming that there is a market which accounts for an economic activity, we avoid the terminological trap suggested above. The particular location of an economic activity may then be analyzed from the standpoint of which factor or factors are so important that obtaining special benefits from it make the existing market sufficient and profitable. Perhaps by concentrating on one segment of the entire market, perhaps by seeking sales to a few segments of the entire market, perhaps by maximizing or minimizing this element, or complying in part with this one or that, the gains obtained from the activity are magnified. Regardless of which factor governs, it is clear that if we assume that "a" market exists, the investigator may analyze the location forces with clear realization that by special location the demand for the firm's product may be maximized, or costs minimized, or some optimum combination of the two secured.

That a certain location might yield better customers, or that more customers are available to the firm at a certain location represents the main sides of maximizing demand (access to markets). In turn, locating near consumers because proximity is an advantage serves as a secondary side of maximizing demand (also considered as access to markets). On its part, cost minimization implies the condition where a certain site offers the lowest possible level of charges. We could, of course, add to these two determinants the alternative possibility that greater personal gratifications might be offered by location at a specific, and sometimes, different place. However, more of this elsewhere. We detail at present the demand factor and include in it the idea of locational interdependence.[2]

The Area and Site Determining Demand Factors

Apart from recognizing that demand is a factor of location in *every instance,* there are two other main instances where the factor *is significant* in theory and where, accordingly, treatment of it is fruitful.

We find in the first important category that significant freight costs on the finished product may combine with a large geographic area of demand to leave more than one market area within which a given kind of plant could be located. Selection of the one area for location instead of some alternative area may be due to the greater "size" of market in the one. Let us say that demand is then an *area-determining* factor of location. In the second instance, we find that after the market area is selected, the particular site

---

[2]For an early analysis of the demand factor, see E. H. Chamberlin, *The Theory of Monopolistic Competition,* 3rd ed. (Cambridge, 1938), Appendix C.

may be chosen on the basis of demand differentials throughout the area. Significantly these differentials arise as firms "jockey for position." When the competition in the industry causes a certain location pattern (*e.g.* heavy localization with slight dispersion), future locators observe sales differentials throughout the market area, and we hold demand to be a *site*-determining factor of location.

Distinction between the area and site components of the demand factor may be scored by examining the reasons for demand differentials over an area. Thus, if geography is a prime factor accounting for differentials in demand over the economic landscape, the area demand factor is defined to exist. If, on the other hand, the actions of competitors, based on demand and cost elasticities among other forces, accounts for and explains the differentials in demand, the site-determining demand factor is defined to prevail. Question immediately arises as to what is meant when we say that geography must be a prime factor?

To answer the question, we hold that area differentials, and hence area demand factor, are evident whenever mountain ranges, waterways, converging transport lines, topography, raw material availability and freight costs involved in shipment, or other geographic features (including all natural resources *in the concept* as well as population concentrations) help shape out readily identifiable market areas *for given products*. These areas (or regions) must be comparatively independent of the particular price and location policies adopted by firms in a given industry. They must, in short, be commonly referred to by people in the trade. Accordingly, even though variations in market area will take place from product to product, regardless of geographic components, and even though we recognize that a given geographic market area is never perfectly hard and fast for any one product, but rather shifts with the very act of location, what controls is whether or not some more or less distinctive areas are considered to exist. If they are, the area demand factor applies to the industry. The location of branch or original plants then reflects, at least, the existence of these alternative market areas. Of course, the site-determining (locational interdependence) demand factor may also be relevant.

When one considers location of plants in a state, the area demand factor may immediately be seen to be of importance. That our survey directs its attention to this aspect of the demand factor may well be anticipated. In turn, whatever inquiries we make into situations where the overall magnitude of demand *within* a given region or market area is altered by the location of a firm and where, accordingly, the site selected by a firm is influenced by the particular places where rivals have located, or might be expected to locate, tend to be special. In any event, our overall concept of the demand factor suggests advantage if we next observe certain distinctions between first plant, relocated plant, or branch location, as well as distinctions between the cases where alternative market areas do or do not exist.

The Three General Types of Plant Location

There are three general types of plant location which must be distinguished before we are able to understand fully the concept "access to markets": (1) a first plant (including a relocation) by a firm where the market is point formed or continuous; (2) a branch plant location due to the development of a distant market; and (3) a first or branch plant location selected after several alternative new market areas have been considered, where at least one of the alternative markets has grown to significant size.

The first type is the one traditionally described in location theory. We consider under it the situation where the market is formed at a point on a map, or over a continuous tract of land, and where, accordingly, there are two main ways in which the demand factor may dominate: (a) Frequently it is important that a manufacturer be located near his buyers in order to be able quickly to adjust specifications to consumers' wishes and to be readily available for consultation. Style goods, such as ladies' hats, are a well-known example. The same sort of situation exists for many technically complicated items, such as missile components. *Comparably*, access is gained by location at places often visited by buyers. Where this factor leads to a location offering close contact with the buyer, the plant is considered to be seeking access to a market. (b) Regionalism, state and local pride, may provide the motivation for a particular location.[3] Should a particular market be

---

[3]See, for example, McLaughlin and Robock, *Why Industry Moves South* (Kindgsport, 1949), p. 37.

Similarly, a leading official of a company in Jacksonville, Florida, notes that local sales advantages are often gained as a result of associations formed by men

highly influenced by a "buy at home" philosophy, it follows that a location in the area may possess advantages on the demand side which prevail apart from other forces.

The second type is described readily by illustration. Suppose the original plant of a firm was located in Connecticut and that this plant was oriented to the Eastern industrial area. Suppose further that a modest amount of total output had for some years been sold in Florida, but that recently the development of the Florida market has caused a relatively expanding part of the output of the Connecticut plant to be earmarked for sale in Florida. In time, either expansion of the original plant or an entirely new plant is indicated. But while the Connecticut plant may have been well oriented to the Pennsylvania, New York and adjacent markets, it may not be particularly well located with respect to Florida or, let us say, the deep South generally. This location shortcoming may be attributable to the high cost of transportation involved, as large savings could be realized by location in or near to Florida, especially if raw materials are available in or near this area. Most important, observe that the market is continuous and the area determining demand factor irrelevant.

The reason for the location of a branch plant might clearly be savings in transport costs, or else labor unrest, high insurance rates, or other disadvantages may in fact prevail at the original plant site. Whatever the actual case may be, in selecting the factors responsible for a branch plant location, the plant locator tends naturally to compare his new branch with his old factory in terms of the market to which the new plant sales are being directed, but not in terms of the respective sizes of the markets. He recognizes, in this way, the demand or market factor for what it usually is, simply a subsidiary factor accounting for the branch plant location.[4]

It is probably the third type of plant location decision which is most common today, as many firms are finding rather suddenly

---

living in the same community and engaged in the same industrial activity. A home-town prejudice adds to better service possibilities and other related advantages gained from close contact. Since such advantages do not accrue to firms located at a distance from the given market, this consideration serves often as a significant factor of location after the overall market has been selected.

[4]In the referenced case, the demand factor would tend to be primary only where location near the buyer is a prerequisite to effective sales promotion (e.g., regional bias in consuming).

that their original plants are both insufficient in size to meet growing demands and improperly located with respect to the new "total
market." A decision to locate a branch plant in one place entails
often a preference for one area extremity over an alternative one,
a preference either as to cost or demand or both. What is important about this is that the locator who seriously considered an alternative location in a different area may be expected to designate
a different set of factors (or forces) as having governed his choice
than would the locator faced with a decision of the second type,
i.e. where no alternative area was considered. Quite often, we may
expect the demand factor to govern his location.

Compared to possible expansion of the original plant, the establishment of a branch plant may offer advantages in transport
or labor costs. On the other hand, compared to location of a branch
plant in an alternative market area, the location selected for the
branch plant may offer more favorable taxes, markets or insurance
rates. The important point is that the advantages in the first case
above may be entirely different from those in the second. And,
going one step further, the results of a spot check among respondents during the survey suggest that locators of branch plants—
where an alternative market area was considered—tend to regard
the main determinant of the particular new location as the factor
which appears most advantageous compared to *the alternative location.* Next, the factor making the branch plant economic compared
to the original plant tends to be listed, in effect being designated
as a secondary or tertiary force.

To summarize, our model must conform to general location
theory in distinguishing between cost, demand and, if desired,
purely personal factors.[5] Further, it must differentiate between first
plant locations (including relocations) and branch location as well
as between first plant or branch plant locations where no alternative
market areas exist and where *there are* alternative market areas.
It is precisely where alternative market areas do exist, and where
second, third, etc. branch plants are involved that the most serious

---

[5]Example, see G. Katona and J. H. Morgan, "The Quantitative Study of
Factors Determining Business Decisions," *Quarterly Journal of Economics,*
LVI (1941-42), pp. 67-90. Also M. L. Greenhut, *Plant Location in Theory and
in Practice* (Chapel Hill, 1956), especially chapter XII.

problems arise in empirical research.[6] And it is in such situations that we must draw a fine distinction between the market and transportation factor.

Market or Transport Cost Advantage on the Finished Product

The changing situations which may produce contradictory answers when one is not armed with an inclusive theoretical system are so complex as to suggest present advantage if we now pause to provide a brief examination of two vital points. We maintain, first, that when transport distance is less in one area than in another, profits will be greater there than elsewhere, *ceteris paribus*. And if the location happens to take place near to the consumer, the orientation is, to be sure, to the market. However, this market orientation is not because of the size of market (or demand) factor; rather, other things being equal, it is because of savings in transport cost. If, second, the distance is found to be less in one area than in another, it may nevertheless be that an even greater advantage lies in forces other than transportation, and among these other forces the most prominent may be the size of market. Manifestly, we must make sure that confusion in selecting between transportation and the market is avoided.

The Problem Considered Further

Suppose the total distance from a plant to its customers is less in one area than in another. If, then, freight cost on the finished product is a significant factor of location, a company official may well visualize his greater profits at the selected location to be attributable to a transport cost saving. But, *in fact*, we shall see that the real advantage might actually lie in its stronger market. By way of suggesting the picture ultimately to be unfolded, it should be realized that if a greater quantity of sales is desired in each market than the amount which served as the basis for our original

---

[6]Probably many would suspect that, at least in the earlier years of the industrial growth of the United States, the location of an original plant was conceived in terms of a total (more or less) nationwide market. The growth of rival market areas, the development of rival firms and rival products, the need for speedy delivery, personalized service, *etc.*, in turn, have caused conception of alternative market areas, possibly even in the case of original plants today. And this particular conception is, of course, part and parcel of the theory of locational interdependence that is stressed in Greenhut, *Plant Location,* especially Chapters II, III, and VI.

supposition (namely, that the total distance from plant to customers is less in the one area than the other), then the transport cost totals may be reversed under this greater amount of sales. As an alternative thought, note that if we simply seek the "same" sales total in the less profitable market as in the more profitable area, the average delivered price in this market may have to be so much less in order to effect this sales total that the derived price differential times the number of units sold would sum up to a greater dollar difference (and hence greater disadvantage) than is the dollar differential between the transport costs on the finished products. Clearly—and we repeat—a fine distinction between the two, as well as specific referential points, must be drawn. Only then will we be able to select consistently among these factors of location.

Separating the Market Factor from Transport Cost on the
Finished Product

Recall first that we are concerned here with the location of a plant or branch plant where there are alternative market areas. This kind of situation raises the possibility of selecting one area rather than another, either because of the market factor or the transport cost factor, assuming further, of course, that other readily identifiable differences, such as labor cost differences, are unimportant.

Let us refer to the one market area as A and the other as B. Consider the price and sales volume which yield greatest profits between the two areas and assume that this holds for area A. Because the profit maximizing output carries a certain average delivered price (AP_A), by determining this price, the basis for comparison with B can be effected.

AP_A must equal the base mill price plus the freight cost on all sales allocated on an average basis to each unit sold. In other words, we must total up all freight cost ($\sum_{i=1}^{n}$ f.c.$_i$, where fc$_i$ stands for the freight cost on the ith unit sold, with i taking on the successive values 1, 2, 3, . . . n, and where n is the total number of units sold) divide by the number of sales (n) and add to the base mill price P to derive AP_A.

$$(1) \quad AP_A = P + 1/n \sum_{i=1}^{n} \text{f.c.}_i$$

Consider the same sales total in B; that is, let n in B be the same as in A. Clearly AP_A may be $\gtreqless$ AP_B. If the same sales total in B yields the same average delivered price as in A, it follows that the greater profits in A must reflect lower costs, possibly in transport. It may be that for equal n, AP_B is lower than AP_A; then, the market in A is stronger than in B.

We may provide a more concrete picture of alternative situations by observing the following. Suppose that under a given physical sales volume, one location yields an income so large that it more than compensates for its cost disadvantages: then the optimum location is market oriented. (This situation, for example, usually prevails for an exclusive retailing shop located at an expensive downtown corner.) If, on the other hand, the same location is better than all others from *both* an income and cost viewpoint, the principal factor is "demand" or "cost," depending on which of these elements contributes more to net income in comparison with the next best alternative location. Last of all, a location may proffer cost advantages and sales disadvantages. (A nonexclusive retailing establishment located at a distance from the downtown area may illustrate a situation where the reduction in unit selling price is more than compensated for by lower land cost and taxes.)

If we find that at the given "n" sales in the profit maximizing market A, and the other market B, the allocation of freight cost in A (*i.e.*, $1/n \sum_{i=1}^{n} f.c._i$) is either greater than, equal to, or not sufficiently less than the greater average delivered price in A over B, the advantage of A over B is a market advantage and not an advantage in the cost of transporting the finished product. (An example of this situation in symbolic form is where

$$1/n \sum_{i=1}^{n} f.c._i \text{ in A} > 1/n \sum_{i=1}^{n} f.c._i \text{ in B while } AP_A > AP_B.)$$

We may generalize beyond transport costs versus market advantage by holding further that, if the average delivered price advantage in the profit maximizing market is sufficiently greater than any cost of production advantage that might also exist (*i.e.* $[AP_A > AP_B] > [C_B - C_A]$, where $C_B > C_A$ (and each C factor stands for material procurement plus processing costs), the governing factor of location is the better market in A compared to B. Combining these arguments may yield a relation such as (2),

$$(2) \quad [1/n \sum_{i=1}^{n} \text{f.c.}_i \text{ in A} - 1/n \sum_{i=1}^{n} \text{f.c.}_i \text{ in B}]$$

$$\gtreqless [AP_A - AP_B] > [C_B - C_A]$$

where a freight cost disadvantage in A compared to B is assumed, and where the first inequality or equality in (2) therefore depends on the relation between P_A and P_B, since, to recall, AP_A is defined

as $P_A + 1/n \sum_{i=1}^{n} \text{f.c.}_i$, and, correspondingly, for AP_B. Or, a re-

lation in which the market is dominant, such as (3), may arise.

$$(3) \quad [1/n \sum_{i=1}^{n} \text{f.c.}_i \text{ in B} - 1/n \sum_{i=1}^{n} \text{f.c.}_i \text{ in A}]$$

$$\lesseqgtr [AP_A - AP_B] > [C_B - C_A]$$

In (3), we see that the freight cost advantage in A is smaller than its market advantage, and, similarly, for the production cost advantage.

Let us realize that demand may be uniform from region to region, but that though the same 'average' delivered price brings forth an identical quantity of sales in the two markets, it may be that, in order to gain these sales in the less profitable region, buyers who are spread out over a greater spatial extent have to be attracted. In this event, transport costs would be high and a transport cost (not market) disadvantage would exist.

Suppose, finally, we observe how judgments of location shift with slight changes in data. For example, assume simply that there are two market areas with the same number of buyers dispersed differently in each, but with each buyer having an identical demand. Assume also the f.o.b. price system. Then, given the same 'average' delivered price, the given quantity may be sold. The difference in profit positions would, accordingly, be attributable to a difference in costs—let us say transport costs. But now imagine that the location of competitors in the already less profitable area limits the market (number of buyers) for a prospective new firm.

To gain the given quantity of sales requires a reduction in the 'average' delivered price. The primary location factor thus may change to that of markets in place of savings in transport costs. Depending on the situation, an equation 3 might prevail, where the freight cost advantage in one place over another is less than its average delivered price advantage, or, of course, an equation 2 might prevail or some equation where the production cost factor is the governing force, etc.

The Market Factor—Case Illustrations

It is probably true that in most situations an enterprise is faced with alternative markets. Selection of a plant site in Florida, if due to considerations other than cost or personal gratifications, must involve the belief that the Florida market is superior (at present or in the near future) to the alternative market. However, note that a company which finds advantage in being located near the consumer cannot necessarily use this factor of proximity to explain its specific location in Florida. Rather, the better market in Florida or cost may have attracted the firm to this state, and then, *given this market,* or the cost advantage, the specific site selected may have been due to the principle of proximity.

Proximity or home-bias serves as the factor which brings a firm to Florida chiefly in the special situation where the market is formed essentially in this State. In effect, Florida constitutes the only market for the particular industry in such a case. The more general situation, however, is where alternative markets exist. Access to markets serves in this general event as the dominant factor when the locating firm considers the Florida market to be superior to others. It is the market, then, which attracts the enterprise to Florida, with the specific location in the State being due to some other force, perhaps labor cost or taxes, or possibly the desire to be near selected consumers, home bias, etc.[7]

---

[7]It should be clear that if firms locate in Florida because the only market exists in Florida, the location in Florida may be due either to what we call access to markets or to costs or personal gratifications. If the former prevails, *i.e.,* access to markets, this means that either proximity or home-bias has dominated the site-selection.

The instructions on the questionnaire to Part II, question 1, and Part III, question 2, are designed to elicit comparable response to the access to market factor from firms that select the Florida market over other alternative markets and from firms that locate in the State because only one market exists and proximity to buyers or home-bias is the vital consideration.

The ways in which one market may be more attractive than another reflect the general situation of its containing customers who are possessed of a greater total demand for the product of a new plant than those in other markets. It need not be a stronger market from the point of view of aggregate demand, but only in so far as concerns a new plant of a particular sort. A series of case models which mirror this general situation will help to clarify these particular propositions and may now be presented.

The Case Models

Firm D has its main location near the center of the national market. It considers establishing a branch plant. By setting up this unit in State B, which forms a fringe part of the entire market area, it can reduce total freight cost on sales in this fringe area. If the sales potential in this fringe area is sufficient to make it possible to establish a plant of a technically efficient size, a branch plant in the fringe area may be economically feasible. This is especially likely to be the case if the product produced by Firm D gains weight in its processing and hence is shipped at higher transport costs than are the raw materials out of which it is made.

In answer to a questionnaire, one spokesman for Firm D claims that access to the particular market constitutes the main locational motivation. Another spokesman for the same firm claims that the site-selection is due to an effort to minimize freight cost. Which is the correct answer?

Observe that the site-selection involves carving a market area out of a larger one. If the firm in question would select this sub-market over any other one which could be carved out of the whole market area, *even if* production costs plus freight costs on the final product for "n" quantity of sales are higher, then, as indicated in our earlier distinction of markets vs. transport cost on the finished product, we accept access to markets as the main factor of location.

If, on the other hand, there is no other sub-market sufficient in size to warrant a branch plant location, or if the firm would locate its branch plant with reference to this market segment, *if and only if* the general cost level is lower than that which exists in other segments, then cost is the main location factor.[8] Significantly, we

---

[8]We might stress here the situation where no alternative market area exists and the particular distant segment in question alone has grown sufficiently in

must realize that in the eventuality discussed in the preceding paragraph, demand is great either because competitors are absent, or because customers are relatively more numerous and have a greater economic want for the product, or because comparable reasons prevail to account for the strong demand. In the instance of this paragraph, cost, not demand, determines the location.[9]

Firm E operates in an industry in which delivered price is the same throughout the United States. The market extends over the whole nation. Firm E locates in State D, claiming that, even though costs of production are high in this state, the absence of competitors near this location enables it to maximize profits. In effect, for a given volume of sales, its production costs plus all freight costs are less than at any other location. It sells this volume to nearby buyers.

The respondent who first described the situation claims that his firm has located to minimize costs. His partner protests and says that "access to markets has governed the location and total costs are minimized only because the absence of competitors enables the given volume of sales to be made to buyers who are located nearby. A small total amount of freight payments takes place in this kind of market."

It is manifest that the second partner has mixed his argument. Certainly, the vital effect of the relative nonexistence of competitors near the selected plant site—under an equalizing delivered price system—is not to change the overall magnitude of demand in the market, but to enable the firm to sell large quantities of its product without having to traffic its goods over long distances. While production costs may be high, sufficient freight costs are saved to leave

---

size to warrant a location with respect to it. In this case, if the proximity to consumers factor is unimportant (that is, if there is no great advantage in, or necessity for being located close to consumers), the basic factor inducing the branch plant location is not access to market but a saving that will be gained in cost, possibly in transporting the finished product. To be sure, market growth can be underscored in a subsidiary role. How respondents to a questionnaire will be instructed to distinguish the alternative conceptions that are possible is discussed in the following section of the chapter.

[9]Contract manufacturers, who, in effect, assemble the parts for the manufacturer, locate in different sectors of a regional or national market. Weight is added in the assembly process, and consequently freight cost is reduced through a scattering of locations. As contract manufacturers for other concerns, they often seek access to particular markets, such as Florida, and cut distributing costs of the product.

the location in State D as the most favorable. The advantage gained is attributable to the shorter transport lines, as the average delivered price is pre-determined for an "n" sales potential, with such sales quantity being possible should the firm seek this end.

Firm G locates in State F. The delivered price for the product of this industry is the same throughout the United States. The spokesman for Firm G claims that rivals and demand are scattered uniformly over the nation, but that the level of unit costs is lower in State F, and hence that costs are the governing elements. His associate disagrees with the twist given by the spokesman. He asserts that at the same total costs (production plus all freight costs), a greater unit volume of sales can be realized through the location at F, and that, therefore, access to markets is the governing factor.

Clearly, any time that the level of production plus transportation costs is lower at one place than another, all other things equal, there will be a greater unit volume of sales at the same total of costs for the firm that benefits from the lower unit cost level. But this greater unit volume of sales, when compared to those attained by a comparable firm subject to higher unit costs, cannot be termed the result of better markets. Nor can a location which gains these cost advantages be considered as one which offers the advantage of access to markets. In every respect, this is a clear case of cost advantages which have the natural effect of tending to yield a greater sales volume. A comparable sales volume, not comparable cost totals, is an easier basis to use in distinguishing the advantages of alternative locations.

Consider Firms S and T. Assume that delivered price is the same throughout all markets. Visualize two homogeneous and equivalent market areas from the standpoint of buyers and buyer locations, respectively to be called markets X and Y. Firm S locates at the material source with respect to market X. Equivalently, Firm T is located somewhere in the market area of market Y. The product loses weight during fabrication, and the freight cost in shipping the final product is less than the freight on the raw materials.

Assume that Firm S can produce and transport its needed raw materials and the final product in such manner that its total cost per unit of distance per unit of product is less than that of Firm T. We would say, as a result, that costs governed the location of S. But then suppose we change the facts only slightly. Suppose we imagine that firm T's spokesman explains that the competition in

S's market X is greater than in T's market Y. Further, he states that though T's processing and transportation costs per unit of product (assuming a unit of product sold at each point in the market) would be greater than that of Firm S, its smaller profit per unit of distance is overbalanced by the much larger number of units that it is able to sell in its market over a smaller distance. In effect, the spokesman claims that his is the *real* least cost location; otherwise phrased, he asserts that his access to markets is better and thereby governed his location. Is his view correct?

Can we not say about the above case that the better transport relations enable a given sales volume at lower total costs even when the basic cost level is higher or the same? In effect, the firm that is poorly located would have to ship outside of its normal sales radius to obtain the same sales total that maximized profits in the otherwise high costing area. If it did this, its freight costs would prove tremendous and its cost level would therefore be the higher. The result of our situation between firms S and T is just about the same as that deduced for firm E.

Making the Theory Operational

Though a rather precise distinction between concepts may be drawn for a theoretical framework, the empirical application of definitions is another matter. How are respondents to a mail questionnaire to be led into a common use of words short of by asking them to read lengthy discourses (which, of course, they would not do) where the terms are defined. Indeed, it may well be that they have a traditional predilection to employ some of the relevant words or phrases in a different way than the researchers. After much struggling with this problem, we arrived at a decision. In turn, we checked this decision several times with different plant officials to assure ourselves that our theory would thereby be made operational.

Basic Language Established

To begin: What we needed was some simple set of words, or should we say as simple a set as possible, which would so instruct respondents as to cause them to apply *our concepts* when completing the questionnaire. The key to the whole problem, as we have already seen, is the concept of a "certain" sales quantity (n) at the profit maximizing location. What was needed was some counterpart word or phrase which is traditionally used by business men. The term sales potential, we found, approached our concept rather closely.

Suppose a businessman is asked to comment on the sales potential he expects to obtain in one market compared to another. What totals will he mentally compare? Will he take net mill price times quantity sold and add freight cost to derive a gross sales receipt, and will he compare this sum with its counterpart in the alternative area? Or will he just consider the net mill price and multiply that by the number of units sold in the profit maximizing area? In turn, will he compare this sum with the receipts expected on a similar (let us say identical) sales quantity at an alternative location?

The answer, we were advised, depends ultimately upon whether the product is sold on a delivered or f.o.b. mill basis. However, because recognition is often given to the alternative transport forms used by buyers (*e.g.*, trucks vs. railroad), the words sales potential would probably suggest to even f.o.b. mill sellers the idea of strength of demand in the market under a given volume of sales. This strength of demand—or let us say total demand—implies total cost to buyers (*i.e.*, total payments made by buyers). It signifies, in turn, that the words "sales potential" would trigger a thought process which at least approximates our concept AP_A times n. Sales potential, we were told, suggests gross sales receipts.

What happens if an alternative market area (or segment, if you prefer) is considered, but actually is poorer than the selected one? Under our theory AP_A is $> AP_B$ for "n" units sold. To business men considering this situation, sales of the same quantity in the poorer market would require a lower delivered price; hence, the sales potential would be lower.

What would happen if, in theory, the markets were identical, but the transport relations differed? Let us say $\sum_{i=1}^{n}$ f.c.$_i$ in A $<$ $\sum_{i=1}^{n}$ f.c.$_i$ in B, but $AP_A = AP_B$. To a businessman, the transport cost level in one area would be lower than another. At the same moment, the sales potential of the alternative market would be the same. In turn, if his mind focused on "some" sales quantity, his sales potential, he would recognize that the distance relations differ and hence transport costs in the market would be different than in the other.

What would happen if, in theory, the markets and transport relations were identical, but procurement of raw materials (including freight cost on the raw materials) and production costs diverged? Clearly, the same sales potential would be visualized by business men, with recognition given to some cost differentials, perhaps labor or power costs, or some others.

Pursuant to these thoughts we instructed respondents to consider the sales potential in the selected market areas before selecting the factors which induced their location. We did this, in effect, by describing briefly a location process in which a market area is selected as the most profitable because of its greater sales potential even though (or even if) its level of cost is higher. (See the questionnaire, instruction to part III-2). We used this kind of wording to avoid any possible "talking-down" to would-be respondents. Comparably, we accepted the thought that any *formal* instructions or definitions would cause disinterest and lessen the response rate. Moreover, we believed our objectives would be met by informal wording.

Observe that *in effect* we challenged the respondent to claim a greater sales potential *if he wanted to select the market factor as having been responsible for his location.* AP_A times "n" would have to be greater than AP_B times "n," *regardless of costs.*

Special Problems.

Several other problems remain which must be discussed, most of which are "illusory," but one of which is real. Among the "illusory" dangers is this situation: What if it is the Southeast market area which is better than the Northwest market area, and, as a consequence, the firm locates a plant in Florida rather than Oregon? More specifically, suppose the Southeast market area is centered in Georgia and South Carolina? Would a respondent be inclined to focus attention on the greater sales volume and hence claim that his Florida location gave him access to markets, or would he recognize some other forces? Of course, with this particular question, we are back to the starting point of our chapter.

Recall that a researcher's focus must change with the objectives of a study. If an investigation is being conducted for, say, "A Southern Governor's Conference," with interest centered in the forces inducing location in the South, the access to market factor would be the correct answer for the location under consideration. But, clearly, it is not *the market* which brought the firm in question to *Florida*. Rather some statewide or local cost advantage induced the firm to locate in the State.

In contrast, suppose the Florida market is the focal market point and the firm locates in Georgia, is there any special problem? Taking the last instance first. A Florida study would not tend to be concerned with a firm which locates in Georgia because the Florida market offered sales volumes advantages; if it did, the location in Georgia would have to be attributed to cost by any reasonably well informed respondent. In comparable manner, a location in Florida, with design to stress sales in the South Carolina (or, let us say, the N.Y.C.) market, would clearly defer to some cost advantage, not the market factor. We suggest that in cases of this kind, respondents would tend to ignore the existence of an alternative market area—*e.g.*, the Northwest market area. They would tend to consider the Southeast market area alone, as if it were the only one. As our background conception of this kind of location situation, we, therefore, visualize the original plant location or a branch plant location where the locational effort seeks to enhance the profitability of sales made to some segment of the overall market. Under this general conception, the problems of the alternative market area case are avoided.

Conclusions

We believe that respondents tend to answer properly directed location survey questions correctly. This kind of response holds even though, from case to case, there may be a difference in whether an original location, a relocation, or a branch location is involved, and whether or not alternative market areas exist. Moreover, we find that for each type of location, the terms markets and costs may have well defined and theoretically significant meanings. Except for the rather infrequent case of great advantages due to proximity to consumers (either in the sense of contact advantages or regional bias), a selection of the access to markets factor implies a location selected after alternative markets have been considered. Selection of a cost factor frequently implies the single market situation, though the recording of the access to market factor in a subsidiary role would, in turn, suggest (probably more often than not) that alternative market areas exist. Indeed, if proximity to buyers does not serve as an important factor, we find, in the referenced situation, that the area of location *generally* possesses advantages with respect to some of the alternative markets considered by the firm. Manifestly, the word *generally* suggests an additional possibility.

To speak explicitly about the additional possibility where access to markets might be referred to as a subsidiary factor even though no alternative market areas exist, what happens, let us ask, when an original plant is located, say in Pittsburgh, and then later on a distant market—the Florida market—grows sufficiently to warrant consideration of a branch location. Assume that the basic industrial location factor is the cost saving possible (in transporting raw materials) when the firm locates at the raw material supply. Assume, further, that an alternative hitherto untapped raw material supply point is available in Florida. What forces induce the Florida location?

Some reflection reveals that the real saving gained by a branch plant in Florida lies not in the cost of transporting the raw materials, for, presumably, the Pittsburgh plant has minimized such cost. Rather, the chief advantage of the Florida location is the transport cost saving on the finished product, *ceteris paribus*. Most interviewees, as well as our other respondents, readily recognized this distinction. They did not consider the freight cost saving on raw materials to be *the* governing factor inducing the location in Florida, although, in cases of this kind, they did select it as the governing location factor in the industry (see Part II of the questionnaire). In fact, it was the difference in answers between Parts II and III of the questionnaire which led us to selected follow-ups of the indicated kind. In many of these instances, the respondents recorded the raw material transport factor as a subsidiary factor in explaining the Florida location, a status they also designated generally for the access to market factor.

Let us note finally, in regard to what we have called our illusory problems, that it is essentially in the alternative market area or proximity to buyer case that the access to market factor would ex-

plain the location in Florida.[10] Most frequently, the better market
in Florida may have attracted the firm to the State and, *in turn*,
the advantage of proximity (or of some cost) may have induced
the particular location, such as in Miami or Orlando. Less frequently was proximity the actual access to market factor that
brought the firm to Florida. In fact, our follow-up phone calls
and interviews revealed it to be relevant *only* in the local sense,
that is, after other forces already induced the acceptance of Florida
as the state for location.

Problems Continued.

This discussion brings us to our second main problem, that of
underscoring the meaning of the personal factor for respondents.
Alas, we decided here that the complexities of the factor could
not really be resolved by instructions or descriptions on a questionnaire. Rather, we decided that, at best, an instruction or description
set would lessen misunderstanding, but ultimately each respondent
who relates his location to the purely personal factor must be visited
and interviewed. Because of this decision, it remains for us only
to explain our theory of the personal factor in plant location—and
for that matter in general economics. We assign the next and con-
cluding section of this chapter to such end.

The Personal Factor

In our previous discussions, we used the terms *governing* or
main factor of location, greatest or *maximum profits,* and a few
others of camparable order. The implication was that the greatest
pecuniary profit explains plant location, and that the factor or
factors most responsible for this greatest profit return may be classified as the governing or main force in the location. But what about
enterprises that do not seek greatest pecuniary profits this month,
this year, this decade, or perhaps at any time? Are they to be ex-
cluded from our theoretical construct, or, to the contrary, are they
to be *included* in the total picture? This broad question of whether
purely personal values may serve as the main factor of location,

---

[10]Bear in mind that the locational interdependence factor may account for
a market orientation in Florida. However, the peninsular layout of the state
suggests that more often than not geography will account for this State's area-
determining factor of location.

and whether they belong to the overall theoretical system as vital parts rather than as exceptions, must be answered.

The Personal Factor And Greatest Profits

The personal element has two main sides. On the one hand, this factor may be tied up with certain economic advantages. On the other hand, it may exist alone, being devoid of all economic content. We find the personal factor tied up with economic gains when a businessman anticipates better relations with his customers, suppliers, bankers, workers, and others, all because of long-standing personal or family acquaintanceship with them. Men with backgrounds in a certain community fall heir to the goodwill which the family (or they themselves alone) have built up. This goodwill provides economic advantages extending from sales to purchases and including ready availibility of capital, good labor relations, and a desirable community attitude. When, however, economic goodwill does not exist in advance of a plant location, the selection of a site for the plant on the basis of personal advantages must mean that some set of personal pleasures which lacked economic content was governing. We should note finally that if a location provides both economic advantages (*e.g.,* access to markets, as defined earlier) and purely personal gratifications, the particular factor that dominated should be distinguished from the one with secondary influence. *And* if the plant locator avers that he would have sought personal gratifications in his site-selection *even if a certain net total of economic disadvantages* were to be experienced at the location, then purely personal gratifications "could be said" to have governed his location. *Our* main interest lies, however, in the economic advantages that may exist in Florida. We distinguish accordingly, the business from the person in all cases, and place central attention on the former.

The Place Of Purely Personal Pleasures in Location Surveys

Notwithstanding our focus, one may wonder how purely personal pleasures fit into a theoretical system designed to explain the functioning of an economy. Indeed, the concern may be magnified by relating it to *our* theoretical system, where, to recall, all basic definitions revolve around the principle of greatest pecuniary profits. Resolution of this problem is fortunately not difficult. The following generalized discussion shows indirectly at first, and then directly, how the two may tie up.

In all location decisions comparisons must be intrapersonal not interpersonal. That is to say, disinterested reporters cannot inquire into the data which molded the decision-making process of one firm on the same basis as they can that which may have controlled another firm. Company resources and hence objectives tend to differ for all. The maximum profit values sought by firm A just cannot be compared exactly with the maximum profit sought by Firm B. Instead, the alternative locations that A considers must be related to its own conception of maximum profits, and not checked with B's conception. The same holds true for B and C, and all others.

Two people, two businessmen, and two firms may share a common desire for greatest profits and yet respond quite differently to alternative activities that offer different profit sums. One enterprise and enterpriser may be conservatively formed; another may be more daring in plans and in deeds. Opposite choices may be made by comparable firms because the material make-up of their personnel differs. We might find that one business unit wants sure bets, while another seeks the lure of greater gain generally commensurate with greater risk. Or, the financial position of one may be such that only a small risk can be taken, whereas another can afford a large risk. In effect, we reach the result that the decision-making process may yield opposite choices, even though the parties of interest claim their desire for the same end: namely, greatest pecuniary profits.

Place a third seller nearby who is more obsessed with a want for security than either of the above two. This seller readily sacrifices higher returns for the safety of an assumed "satisfactory" profit. Whether or not each seeks to optimize over a month, a year, a biennium or perhaps a greater period of time, does not matter. What is alone significant is the fact that if conditions of certainty (not risk and/or uncertainty) prevailed in the world of business, a fixed maximum profit point would be identifiable, and any selection of a lower value would be noneconomic. Seen from the opposite side, where risk and/or uncertainty dominate the economic landscape, a range of probable values arises which leaves room in the process of decision-making for conservative businessmen to select one location and activity, and for more daring tradesmen to select another. Each person represents, in his own way, the economic man.

Consider, finally, the fact that a noneconomic decision may prevail and be identifiable. We shall use a rather elementary pattern to demonstrate further our thoughts.

Suppose several sellers compute their profit prospects at alternative locations and derive similar values. But imagine that, among them, one is completely security minded. He notes that at the otherwise best location there exists a possible (albeit unlikely) profit result which is exceedingly bad. Though, we assume, businessmen in general would ignore the "possible" bad result, because its happening is so unlikely, our security-minded seller rejects the location on this ground. Whatever site *he* next selects is attributable then to the personal factor.

We define *the purely personal factor of location* to be operative when the noneconomic gratifications of the individual (gamble, security instinct, or, let us now say, psychic satisfactions) so dominated the profit values as to cause the selection of a site different from that which an economic man would have selected. How, it must then be asked, do we decide whether an individual is just a conservative businessman or an extremely security-minded individual? How do we select between a gambler and a daring business man?

In any survey, the opinion of the spokesman must govern. Moreover, it is vital in understanding the statistics presented later for the reader to know this: Many of our respondents did check the personal factor as having governed their location. However, follow-up interviews with each of these persons, and detailed explanation that we were examining the location of the business and not necessarily *the individual,* led to our being told to change many of the original responses of this kind. That conservatism or daring reflects economic behavior, while, in contrast, a penchant for sunshine, or a strong concern with an *unlikely* windfall (profit or loss) amounts to the purely personal factor, was readily understood. In fact, we found that the purely personal factor was instrumental only in causing Florida-bound plants to locate in particular corners of Florida; it was not instrumental in bringing them to the State. According to our respondents and spokesmen, the cost or demand factors attracted new industry to Florida. Only in a few cases was the attraction of the family home or of surf and sunshine overwhelming. Only rarely did it induce an entrepreneur to locate his business in a particular city which seemed to proffer less attractive financial return than that conjectured for another place in Florida.

Summary

We have noted that location factors lie on three levels: the demand factors, the cost factors, and the purely personal factor. We have observed that the personal factor may have an economic connotation, or it may not. Sometimes, because of personal contacts, sales may be enhanced or costs may be reduced. Sometimes, the personal factor may be prevalent in its own right. When the factor is distinct from sales and cost advantages, we refer to it as the purely personal factor of location.

We have reached, then, a point where the terms used in our questionnaire should have attained a common meaning. As a fundamental principle, we might observe that all best locations offer lowest costs at the output that offers greatest profits, or, alternatively, all best locations offer greater sales receipts relative to a given total of costs at the output of greatest profits than do other locations.

When we refer to costs or markets as the main factor governing a plant location, we are simply looking at the same coin from opposite sides. It follows that if a researcher on plant location fails to establish the way he will look at the coin, he subjects himself to the meaningless hodgepodge which becomes part of so many empirical investigations. One tends to find that each person (interviewee, interviewer, respondent, or analyst) converses in his own language, and the requisite common terminology is never brought about. Statistical findings, therefore, mean whatever the reader wants them to mean (or thinks they were supposed to mean). To establish, and then to gain concurrence in definitions, is a laborious task, both for the writer and the reader. Nonetheless, it is completely vital.

The reasons thus have been given why we have taken pains in this chapter to emphasize and to re-emphasize the situations where given words tend to acquire different meaning to different people. There remains the need for observing that concepts are relevant and become significant only as they form some vital part of a theoretical system, for a theoretical system is necessary to *explain* why things happen the way they do. Words, phrases, case studies, and statistics which fall outside of a theoretical framework must fail to enlighten; they are meaningless and reveal nothing. To appreciate location factors for a plant, firm, or industry, to feel the significance of the location forces in a community, state, region, and nation, one must have a theoretical construct in mind. Such a construct, as recorded in this chapter, served as the focal point for our common use of words and hence our survey. Through it, the statistical data acquired in the survey become significant.

CHAPTER IV

STATISTICAL PROCEDURE FOR LOCATION STUDY

The basic information used in the survey was the Florida Development Commission's list of new industrial plants and major expansions for 1956 and 1957. The unadjusted number of plants on this list totaled 1294.

In the interest of economy, a 20 per cent sample of plants believed to have fewer than 100 employees and located in the urban counties was utilized. This sample was selected by the Florida Development Commission. However, a complete (100%) canvass was made of all new plants believed to have over 100 employees and of smaller plants if they located in the counties classified by the Commission as "underdeveloped." All of the plants covered by these categories were sent the questionnaire, the number canvassed being 400. As many as three follow-up letters were sent out per plant in order to build up the response rate. Follow-up letters were also employed extensively in order to clear up answers. In addition, a large number of plants were visited by representatives of the Department of Economics of the Florida State University in order to bring back or to check completed questionnaires. Finally, telephone calls were made to check responses, and a telephone survey was made of non-respondents in order to determine whether the plants of the non-respondents had locational factors similar to those which responded more readily. The telephone survey and the on-the-spot survey revealed, among other things, that many of the non-respondents were no longer in business.

Letters were sent to the tax collectors in every county, and from the replies it was possible to secure more complete addresses and to learn about other cases of discontinuation of operations. A substantial number of relatively lengthy interviews were held with industrialists in new plants in Florida in order to secure a greater depth of knowledge than is possible from any questionnaire survey. Such "interviews in depth" helped to disclose several types of information which could not be anticipated in devising the questionnaire.

Table 1 gives a summary picture of the number and type of firms surveyed and the response rate. A firm is defined as responding if a useable questionnaire was returned directly by the firm or if such a questionnaire could be filled out by means of a personal or telephone interview. In a number of cases it was impossible to secure any useable response for reasons of military secrecy.

TABLE 1.

Response to Questionnaire

Category of Plant	Number of Question- naires Sent Out	Number of Responses	No. Known to Be Out of Business or Inappli- cable	Percent of Response of Eligible Plants
100 or More Emp. Total	107	84	23	100%
Urban Counties	87	67	20	100%
Underdeveloped Counties	20	17	3	100%
25-99 Employees — Total	52	44	6	97%
Urban Counties	24	20	4	100%
Underdeveloped Counties	28	24	2	94%
0-24 Employees — Total	241	133	57	79%
Urban Counties	128	74	22	75%
Underdeveloped Counties	113	59	35	83%
All Plants	400	261	85	83%
Urban Counties	239	161	45	83%
Underdeveloped Counties	161	100	40	83%

A source of great satisfaction was the 100 per cent response rate secured from plants employing, or expected to employ, 100 persons or more. From the 107 questionnaires sent out to these large plants 84 useable responses were secured, but the other 23 were found to be out of business or otherwise inapplicable. For example, some firms postponed their plans for Florida plants due to the 1957-58 business recession, a few moved to other states, and some respondents were found either to have completed their facilities prior to 1956 or to have taken no steps to begin construction until 1958. After removal of 23 plants which did not appear to constitute a proper part of the group to be surveyed, a total of 67 large plants (100 or more employees) remained in the urban counties, and 17 remained in the underdeveloped counties. All of these 84 plants co-operated in the survey.

An outstanding response rate of 97% was secured for plants in the 25 to 99 employee range, after adjustment for those no longer in business or otherwise inapplicable. Only two plants in this size range failed to respond. As indicated earlier, such non-response may actually be based on the top secret nature of the work of some new facilities.

The lowest response rate (75%) was secured from small plants (under 25 employees) in the urban counties. Small plants in the rural counties had an 83% response rate, but it was found that a rather large number of such plants (35) are no longer in business or are otherwise inapplicable.

In order to make the answers of respondents correspond as closely as possible to the "universe," namely, to all applicable plants which located in Florida in 1956 and 1957, a double "blow up" of results was made. First, an adjustment was made for non-respondents. Since a telephone survey of such plants revealed no apparent difference between their locational factors and those of respondents, it was considered most nearly appropriate to fill in locational factors for such non-respondents on the basis of the answers given by the most similar firms which did respond.[1] Also, since a 20 per cent sample was used for plants with less than 100 employees in urban counties, all results for such plants (whether they responded or were "dubbed in") were weighted by five. As a consequence of these statistical procedures all results shown can be considered to be applicable to the entire group of new industrial plants which located in Florida in 1956 and 1957 or in which major expansions occurred, insofar as these plants were still in business during the first half of 1958 when the survey was conducted.

---

[1]The most similar firms were derived first by selecting companies producing the same product that were located in the same or nearest comparable county. Among these companies, those which were nearest in size and then in year of origin were selected. In case more than one concern of similar kind existed, the location factors that were selected for the non-responding firm were decided on the basis of most common agreement or else on experience. In cases of doubt, a phone call or an on-the-spot survey was made, thereby causing the erstwhile non-responding concern to appear on the list of replying firms.

CHAPTER V

GENERAL FINDINGS OF FLORIDA SURVEY

The statistical procedures of our survey were set forth in Chapter IV. Now we present an analysis of the responses made by the businessmen who were contacted, along with some case material wherever relevant.

Number and Types of New Plants

About four times as many new plants are treated in this report as having begun operations in 1957 as in 1956 (605 vs 147). In part this is due to the late reports received by the Florida Development Commission on 124 plants (nearly all of them small) which began operations in 1956 but were reported in 1957. Also, since the survey was conducted in early 1958, most of the 1957 newcomers were still in business, whereas a number of the smaller plants that opened up in 1956 were not. The recession which began in the summer of 1957 was undoubtedly an important contributing factor.

The same factors help explain why the 147 surveyed plants that were started in 1956 provided 22,101 new jobs, as shown in Table 1, compared with 12,006 provided by the larger number of new plants credited to 1957. In addition and most important, many of the latter had not reached their planned employment by early 1958.

Despite the offsetting conditions noted above, it seems to be true that the plants which started in 1956 were larger than the 1957 facilities. As shown in Table 1, 39 plants employing 100 or more persons were located in 1956, while only 23 such plants are shown for 1957. A much larger number of plants with fewer than 25 employees are shown for 1957 than for 1956—516 versus 79. The great increase in new small plants is more marked in South and Central Florida than in the Northern section.

Location of the New Plants

Measured in terms of new employment provided, Northern, Central, and South Florida fared about equally well in the two-year period covered by the survey. As shown in Table 1 total new employment was 11,798 in Region 1 (North), 11,416 in Region 2 (Central), and 10,893 in Region 3 (South). The number of new plants was greatest in the Southern region (377), second greatest

TABLE 1.
Number and Size of Plants by Employee Totals Located by Regions and by Developed or Underdeveloped County in 1956 and 1957 — Adjusted.

	Number of Plants		0-24		25-99		100-499		500 & over		Total Employees		Grand Total
	1956	1957	1956	1957	1956	1957	1956	1957	1956	1957	1956	1957	Total
Region No. 1 (North)													
Developed	29	52	20	45	1	5	7	2	1	0	7,318	1,125	8,443
Underdeveloped	31	38	15	31	9	5	6	2	1	0	2,490	865	3,355
Total	60	90	35	76	10	10	13	4	2	0	9,808	1,990	11,798
Region No. 2 (Central)													
Developed	38	159	17	144	6	9	11	6	4	0	8,442	1,991	10,433
Underdeveloped	3	25	0	19	2	3	1	3	0	0	215	768	983
Total	41	184	17	163	8	12	12	9	4	0	8,657	2,759	11,416
Region No. 3 (South)													
Developed	41	323	26	273	7	41	7	7	1	2	3,425	6,947	10,372
Underdeveloped	5	8	1	4	4	3	0	1	0	0	211	310	521
Total	46	331	27	277	11	44	7	8	1	2	3,636	7,257	10,893
Total All Regions	147	605	79	516	29	66	32	21	7	2	22,101	12,006	34,107

Number of Plants and Employee Totals by Developed or Underdeveloped County in 1956 and 1957.

	Number of Plants		Number of Employees		
	1956	1957	1956	1957	Total
Underdeveloped Counties	39	71	2,916	1,943	4,859
Developed Counties	108	534	19,185	10,063	29,248
	147	605	22,101	12,006	34,107

in the Central section (225), and smallest in the Northern part of the State (150). It is evident that the plants are smaller the further south they are located. In large part this is because the more northerly plants are often designed to supply regional or national markets, while those to the south are usually geared to local markets.

Tables 2, 3, and 4 also show the numbers of plants of various sizes, and the new employment created, by county, for the three regions. In the North, Escambia and Duval counties led in new jobs; Pinellas and Orange counties led in the Central region, while Dade and Broward led in the South. The under-developed counties of North Florida seemed to make somewhat better progress than the rural counties in the other two sections, both in total new jobs created and in average new jobs per county.

Types of New Industry

Distinct differences are apparent in Table 5 in the types of industries locating in the three regions of the State. The chemical industry is locating primarily in Northern Florida (especially the extreme Northwest) with 14 new plants being listed. Central Florida added 10 new plants in this category and South Florida only one. Fabricated metal products show an opposite pattern, with 54 plants in the Southern part of the State, 27 in the middle region, and 23 in the North. The fabrication of aluminum sheets into windows, screens, and other items used in construction is especially noticeable in the populated urban areas. Similarly, the manufacturing of machinery, other than electrical machinery, has developed rapidly in the Southern and Central regions. Many of these plants manufacture precision parts for incorporation by other firms in their products.

Central Florida led in the initiation of new manufacturing of electrical machinery, equipment, and supplies. Many of these plants produce electronic items associated with guided missiles or aircraft. Closely related is the manufacture of professional, scientific, and controlling instruments. Such plants were also located primarily in Central Florida, as is the frozen fruit concentrate industry.

The Northern counties had a good record in the establishment of new lumber mills and wood products plants other than furniture, adding 27 facilities of this sort. Furniture and fixtures manu-

TABLE 2

Number and Size of Plants (by Employee Totals)
Locating in Region 1 by Counties in 1956 and 1957—Adjusted

Counties	Number of Plants		0-24		25-99		100-499		500 and over		Number of Employees		
	1956	1957	1956	1957	1956	1957	1956	1957	1956	1957	1956	1957	Total
Developed Counties													
Clay	1	0	0	0	0	0	1	0	0	0	200	0	200
Duval	20	32	15	25	1	5	4	2	0	0	710	1020	1730
Putnam	1	5	0	5	0	0	1	0	0	0	148	30	178
Escambia	6	15	5	15	0	0	0	0	1	0	6010	75	6085
St. Johns	1	0	0	0	0	0	1	0	0	0	250	0	250
Totals in Developed Counties	29	52	20	45	1	5	7	2	1	0	7318	1125	8443
Underdeveloped Counties													
Alachua	1	4	0	4	0	0	1	0	0	0	400	5	405
Bay	2	0	0	0	1	0	1	0	0	0	150	0	150
Columbia	4	2	1	2	2	0	1	0	0	0	220	8	228
Dixie	3	0	1	0	1	0	1	0	0	0	154	0	154
Gadsden	1	2	0	1	1	1	0	0	0	0	85	50	135
Gulf	1	1	0	0	1	1	0	0	0	0	40	58	98
Hamilton	0	1	0	1	0	0	0	0	0	0	0	13	13
Holmes	2	2	1	2	1	0	0	0	0	0	49	15	64
Jackson	5	1	3	1	2	0	0	0	0	0	153	7	160
Lafayette	0	3	0	3	0	0	0	0	0	0	0	10	10
Lake	1	5	0	4	0	1	1	0	0	0	200	81	281
Leon	0	2	0	1	0	1	0	0	0	0	0	70	70
Levy	1	1	1	1	0	0	0	0	0	0	3	22	25
Liberty	0	1	0	0	0	0	0	1	0	0	0	144	144
Nassau	0	6	0	6	0	0	0	0	0	0	0	17	17
Okaloosa	3	2	3	1	0	1	0	0	0	0	33	81	114
Santa Rosa	1	1	0	0	0	0	1	1	0	0	300	244	544
Suwannee	1	1	0	1	1	0	0	0	0	0	25	12	37
Taylor	2	1	0	1	0	0	1	0	1	0	630	15	645
Union	0	1	0	1	0	0	0	0	0	0	0	5	5
Wakulla	0	1	0	1	0	0	0	0	0	0	0	8	8
Walton	1	0	1	0	0	0	0	0	0	0	18	0	18
Washington	2	0	2	0	0	0	0	0	0	0	30	0	30
Totals Underdeveloped Counties	31	38	13	31	10	5	7	2	1	0	2490	865	3355
TOTAL	60	90	33	76	11	10	14	4	2	0	9808	1990	11798

TABLE 3

Number and Size of Plants (By Employee Totals) Locating in Region 2 by Counties in 1956-1957—Adjusted

Counties	Number of Plants		0-24		25-99		100-499		500 & over		Number of Employees		
Under-developed	1956	1957	1956	1957	1956	1957	1956	1957	1956	1957	1956	1957	Total
Developed													
Brevard	5	24	1	24	1	0	3	0	0	0	600	160	760
Hillsborough	4	27	1	20	2	5	1	2	0	0	233	440	673
Orange	3	21	0	20	2	1	0	0	1	0	3154	177	3331
Pinellas	22	48	15	45	0	0	5	3	2	0	3160	700	3860
Polk	2	16	0	15	1	0	0	1	1	0	1035	225	1260
Seminole	0	3	0	0	0	3	0	0	0	0	0	110	110
St. Lucie	1	0	0	0	0	0	1	0	0	0	150	0	150
Volusia	1	20	0	20	0	0	1	0	0	0	110	179	289
Totals in Developed Counties	38	159	17	144	6	9	11	6	4	0	8442	1991	10433
Citrus	0	2	0	2	0	0	0	0	0	0	0	8	8
DeSoto	0	4	0	2	0	1	0	1	0	0	0	266	266
Flagler	0	1	0	1	0	0	0	0	0	0	0	9	9
Hardee	0	1	0	1	0	0	0	0	0	0	0	11	11
Hernando	0	2	0	0	0	1	0	0	0	0	0	242	242
Indian River	0	4	0	3	0	1	0	1	0	0	0	57	57
Marion	2	4	0	4	1	0	1	0	0	0	185	30	215
Osceola	1	3	0	3	1	0	0	0	0	0	30	19	49
Pasco	0	3	0	2	0	0	0	1	0	0	0	120	120
Sumter	0	1	0	1	0	0	0	0	0	0	0	6	6
Totals Under-developed Counties	3	25	0	19	2	3	1	3	0	0	215	768	983
Total	41	184	17	163	8	12	12	9	4	0	8657	2759	11416

TABLE 4.

Number and Size of Plants (By Employee Totals) Locating in Region 3 by Counties in 1956-1957—Adjusted

Counties	Number of Plants		0-24		25-99		100-499		500 & over		Number of Employees		
Developed	1956	1957	1956	1957	1956	1957	1956	1957	1956	1957	1956	1957	Total
Broward	8	71	0	60	5	10	3	1	0	0	1150	1242	2392
Dade	18	182	15	160	1	15	1	5	1	2	1460	4930	6390
Manatee	0	9	0	8	0	0	0	1	0	0	0	200	200
Martin	1	5	1	5	0	0	0	0	0	0	5	20	25
Palm Beach	11	41	10	25	0	16	1	0	0	0	300	300	600
Sarasota	3	15	0	15	1	0	2	0	0	0	510	255	765
Totals in Developed Counties	41	323	26	273	7	41	7	7	1	2	3425	6947	10372
Under-developed													
Charlotte	0	2	0	1	0	0	0	1	0	0	0	127	127
Collier	1	1	1	1	0	0	0	0	0	0	20	6	26
Glades	0	1	0	0	0	1	0	0	0	0	0	40	40
Lee	4	4	0	2	4	2	0	0	0	0	191	137	328
Total in Under-developed Counties	5	8	1	4	4	3	0	1	0	0	211	310	521
Total	46	331	27	277	11	44	7	8	1	2	3636	7257	10893

TABLE 5.

Plants by Industry Groups, Region, and Years

Industry Type	1956				1957				1956-57
	Total	Region 1	Region 2	Region 3	Total	Region 1	Region 2	Region 3	Total
Metal mining	0	0	0	0	1	1	0	0	1
Mining and quarrying of nonmetallic minerals except fuels	3	1	0	2	4	0	4	0	7
Construction—special trade contractors	0	0	0	0	6	1	5	0	6
Ordnance and accessories	2	0	2	0	0	0	0	0	2
Food and kindred products	39	18	15	6	28	2	9	17	67
Textile and mill products	1	1	0	0	13	0	1	12	14
Apparel and other finished products made from fabrics and other materials	2	1	1	0	20	5	0	15	22
Lumber and wood products, except furniture	14	8	5	1	58	19	9	30	72
Lumber and fixtures	4	3	1	0	33	2	11	20	37
Paper and allied products	4	3	1	0	10	5	0	5	14
Printing, publishing and allied industries	10	0	0	10	52	11	16	25	62
Chemicals and allied products	5	5	0	0	20	9	10	1	25
Petroleum refining and related products	0	0	0	0	12	0	5	7	12
Rubber and miscellaneous plastics products	1	0	0	1	0	0	0	0	1
Leather and leather products	10	0	0	10	5	0	0	5	15
Stone, clay, and glass products	8	3	1	4	42	3	4	35	50
Primary metal industries	1	1	0	0	10	0	5	5	11
Fabricated metal products, except ordnance, machinery, and transportation equipment	13	11	2	0	91	12	25	54	104
Machinery, except electrical	1	0	1	0	81	1	33	47	82
Electrical machinery, equipment, and supplies	8	1	4	3	26	0	17	9	34
Transportation equipment	11	4	3	4	47	10	7	30	58
Professional, scientific, and controlling instruments; photographic and optical goods; watches and clocks	1	0	1	0	19	0	17	2	20
Miscellaneous manufacturing industries	5	0	0	5	18	2	6	10	23
Motor freight transportation and warehousing	0	0	0	0	5	5	0	0	5
Wholesale trade	0	0	0	0	1	0	0	1	1
Miscellaneous services	4	0	4	0	3	2	0	1	7
	147	60	41	46	605	90	184	331	752

facture followed the population, however, being located primarily in the South and Central counties.

Food and kindred products plants appeared in substantial and nearly equal number in all three regions. Printing and publishing plants located in all three sections, but the number of new establishments was substantially greater in the Southern part of Florida.

Considering all industries and all new companies, an unmistakable emphasis on the Florida markets appears. This emphasis is clearly revealed in Figure 1, where we find that more than half of the new plants in the State consider Florida to constitute their principal market. In turn, Figure 2 shows the diverse uses to which the products of Florida's new industry are put.

Summary of Location of New Plants and Types of Industry

We may summarize the main points that were noted in previous paragraphs for the purpose of providing a concise review of vital data at this time as well as to form a reference point for the selected case illustrations which will follow:

(1)   It was noted that the more northerly points tend to supply regional or national markets, while those to the south are geared to local markets.

(2)   Fabricated metal products catering to the construction trade are tending to concentrate in South Florida.

(3)   Electrical machinery, equipment, and supply companies are localizing in Central Florida.

(4)   Lumber mills and wood products plants have been oriented to raw material supply points in the north and south.

Selected Case Examples of the Location of New Plants and Types of Industry

(1)   That the more northerly plants supply regional or national markets reflects in part the transport cost saving that is possible by location in northern Florida. Thus the Chemstrand Company, which manufactures nylon filament yarns in its Northwest Florida plant, was located there in part to hold down the transportation cost in the chemical portion of its operation. At the same time, the company kept the transport cost on its finished yarn within reasonable bounds by locating there rather than in the states farther to the West.

Fig. 1
Principal Market Areas

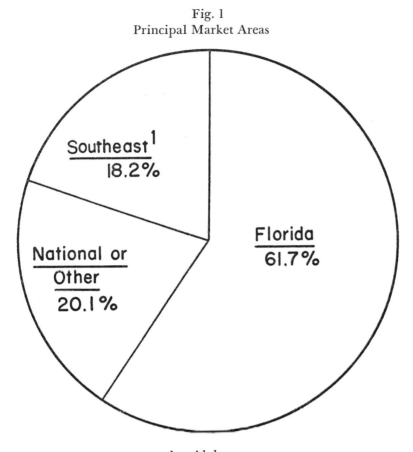

1. Alabama
2. Georgia
3. South Carolina
4. North Carolina
5. Mississippi
6. Louisiana
7. Maryland

[1]Southeastern States, other than Florida Ranked by Number of times Cited as a Market Area

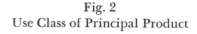

Fig. 2
Use Class of Principal Product

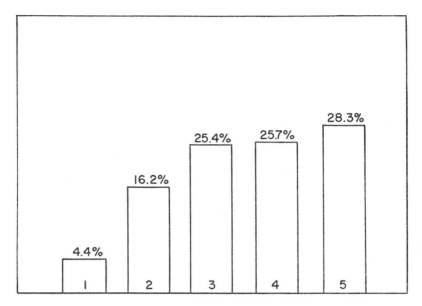

1. For Household Use After Further Processing.
2. For Household Use Without Further Processing
3. Other
4. For Industrial Use
5. For Construction Use

The Florida plant of the Chemstrand Company is unique in the
nylon industry because it produces the nylon filament yarns in
one complete operation: from the basic chemical side to actual
fiber making and packaging.

Chemstrand officials feel that their location in the Pensacola
area holds down reasonably well the freight cost on the chemical
portion of their business. The principal raw materials, cyclohexane
and ammonia, are processed from sources in Texas and Louisiana.
Freight costs on these materials are, therefore, reasonably low.
Though freight cost on the yarn to the textile mills would be lower
from locations in the Carolinas or Virginia, for example, the econo-

mies gained on raw material deliveries, coupled with the gains made possible by a wholly unified operation in Florida, offset the rather high delivery cost of yarn. Transportation, while an important factor, is, of course, only one element in determining the optimum location for such a facility.

Somewhat similarly, the unique Foley branch plant of the Buckeye Cellulose Company was located to be near the company's raw material supply. This firm manufactures cellulose. Because the raw material it uses loses weight and bulk in fabrication, it is cheaper to transport the finished product over long distances than the raw material. Given this basic characteristic, it remained for the company to find a site at which adequate waste disposal facilities were possible and where a sufficient supply of water was available.

(2) The tendency of the fabricated metal products industry to follow the construction industry is readily illustrated by the Adapto Steel Products Company of Miami. The president of this firm desired to isolate a small portion of the national market for steel shelving. Observation showed that Miami, because of its metropolitan nature and rapid growth, comprised a promising market. The spokesman pointed out that at the time of his location the Miami area was served chiefly by distant competitors. But customers prefer to buy from local producers because a local producer will install the final product and should be better able to supply the buyer readily on short notice. These considerations cause firms of this type to select the best available market area that can be found and then to locate at the center of gravity of this area.

(3) The Minute Maid Company of Leesburg, Auburndale, and Plymouth and the Evans Properties of Dade City stress three vital gains from location in Central Florida. One, transport costs on raw materials are minimized. Two, the operation of company-owned groves is maintained at high standards as a result of the easy surveillance that is possible when the main plant is located nearby. Indeed, the ready availability of raw materials which follows from an integrated operation of this kind is a vital consideration and advantage. Three, the citrus codes of Florida and the Federal Marketing Acts require that higher grade fruits be shipped out of Florida to other states. Location, for example, in South Georgia would therefore involve higher priced fruits as well as high freight rates on these perishable raw materials.

Special Findings (Plant Types and the "Whys" of Location)

Branch Plants

It is interesting to note that a very significant number of the new plants established in Florida in 1956 and 1957 were plants of firms which also have facilities in other states. This is especially true of the larger plants.

Table 6 shows that 245 branch plants were established in the state. This compares with 367 plants of new firms. Among plants with less than 100 employees, the new firms dominated, but 26 branch plants with 100 or more employees were established compared with 18 plants of this size belonging to new companies.

The largest number of branch plants appeared in the non-electrical machinery and fabricated metal products fields. These fields also attracted large numbers of new firms.

TABLE 6.

Branch Plants Established in Florida, 1956-57

Industry	Number of Employees				
	0-24	25-99	100-499	500 & over	All Sizes
Metal mining	1	0	0	0	1
Mining and quarrying of non-metallic minerals, except fuels	2	1	0	0	3
Ordnance and accessories	0	0	0	1	1
Food and kindred products	13	1	1	1	16
Textile mill products	0	1	1	0	2
Apparel & similar products	15	0	1	0	16
Lumber and wood products except furniture	8	1	0	0	9
Furniture and fixtures	16	2	0	0	18
Paper and allied products	5	1	1	1	8
Chemicals and allied products	1	2	1	1	5
Petroleum refining and related industries	1	0	0	0	1
Stone, clay, and glass products	16	3	4	0	23
Fabricated metal products	27	0	1	0	28
Machinery, except electrical	37	6	0	0	43
Electrical machinery, equipment, and supplies	15	2	1	1	19
Transportation equipment	11	3	5	1	20
Professional controlling instruments, photographic and optical goods, watches, and clocks	10	1	1	0	12
Miscellaneous manufacturing industries	5	10	0	0	15
Miscellaneous services	1	1	3	0	5
Totals	184	35	20	6	245

The printing and publishing industry contrasts interestingly with the apparel industry in that 46 new independent establishments appeared in the former while no branch plants were set up. In the apparel industry 16 branch plants were set up, while no new firms were counted.

Relocations of Plants

An interesting phase of American economic history deals with the movement of textile mills from New England to the South. Most of Florida's new plants have been established without disturbing those in other states, but a number of relocations from out of state are occurring, especially of small plants. Often a *contributing* reason is that the owner wants to move to Florida.

In all industry groups there were 22 plants employing 25 or more persons which have moved to Florida from other states. Among these were eight plants with 100 or more employees in the "electrical machinery, equipment, and supplies" industry. In part this trend reflects the rapid development of Florida as a center for missile production and testing. Data on relocations from out of state are given in Table 7.

TABLE 7.
Relocation in Florida of Out-of-State Plants: 1956-57
(Number Relocated)

Industry	Number of Employees				
	0-24	25-99	100-499	500 & over	All Sizes
Construction	5	0	0	0	5
Ordnance and accessories	1	0	0	0	1
Food and kindred products	15	1	2	0	18
Textile mill products	5	0	1	0	6
Apparel and similar products	0	0	1	0	1
Lumber and wood products, except furniture	16	0	0	0	16
Printing, publishing, and related industries	5	0	0	0	5
Chemicals and allied products	2	2	1	0	5
Stone, clay, and glass products	1	0	0	0	1
Fabricated metal products	6	0	0	0	6
Machinery, except electrical	5	0	0	0	5
Electrical machinery, equipment and supplies	0	0	7	1	8
Transportation equipment	1	0	0	0	1
Motor freight transportation and warehousing	0	5	0	0	5
Wholesale trade	1	1	0	0	2
Totals	63	9	12	1	85

A total of 55 new plants were found to be relocations from one site in Florida to another. Although 45 of these were small plants, the rather large number points out a pitfall that exists when one counts the employee totals of these concerns as if they add to the net employment in the State. Figure 3 portrays the relative numerical importance of the new firms, branch plants, and in and out of state plant relocations.

The Factors of Location

A summary view of the frequency with which various factors were cited as the most influential in causing location in Florida is provided in Figure 4. Access to markets stands out as the primary factor for slightly over half of the firms surveyed. Expected growth of markets, a closely related factor, was mentioned next most frequently. On the cost side, low freight cost on shipping the final product and on obtaining raw materials stand out.

The relative frequency with which various factors were cited as of second greatest importance is portrayed graphically in Figure 5. Climate as it affects operations and as an attraction to top management shows up much more as a secondary factor than as a primary factor. Figure 6 indicates the relative number of times that factors were cited as of either first or second importance to the decision to locate in Florida.

Factors by Industry

Tables 8, 9, 10, and 11 show the frequency with which the various factors were cited as of first, second, or third greatest importance in the various industries.

(A) The printing and publishing industry, for example, is clearly one which should be near to the consumer because of contact advantages and need for speedy delivery. In practically every case, this factor served as the main cause for selecting the specific community in Florida. But whether the Florida market is superior to other markets in the country, or whether the cost level is lower or whether purely personal considerations caused the shop to be located in the State is another matter. Generally the respondents for this industry ventured the opinion that the Florida market was and is most enticing. It is clear that, theoretically, this is the correct response.

Fig. 3
Type of Plant

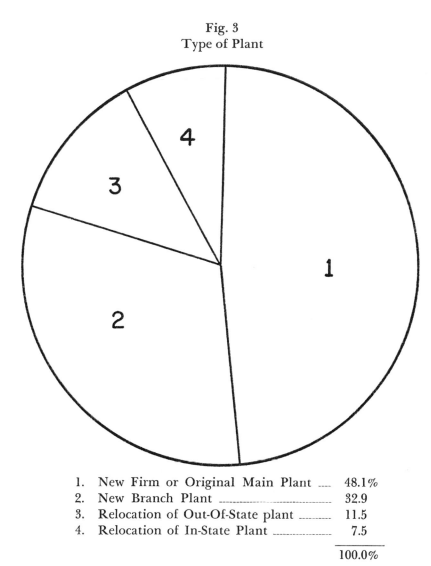

1. New Firm or Original Main Plant ___ 48.1%
2. New Branch Plant _____ 32.9
3. Relocation of Out-Of-State plant _____ 11.5
4. Relocation of In-State Plant _____ 7.5
                                          _____
                                          100.0%

Fig. 4

Percentage of Firms Citing Various Factors as the Most Influential
in Their Florida Location

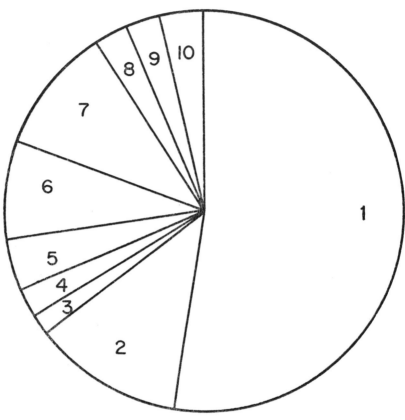

1.	Access to markets	51.9%
2.	Anticipation of growth of markets	12.8
3.	Amicable labor relations	1.7
4.	Lower wages	2.6
5.	Ease of attracting out-of-state personnel, incl. research	4.7
6.	Low freight cost on obtaining raw materials and components	7.7
7.	Low freight cost on shipping final product	10.7
8.	Climate, as it affects operations	1.8
9.	Community facilities (education, police, medical, fire)	2.9
10.	All other factors	3.2

100.0%

Fig. 5
Percentage of Firms Citing Various Factors as Secondarily
Important in Their Florida Location

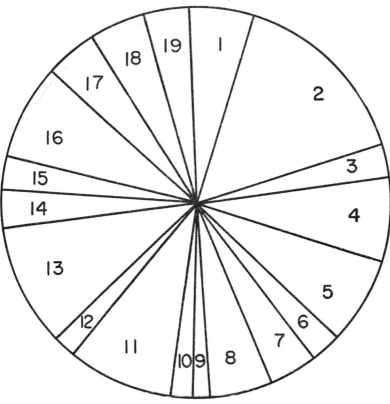

1.	Access to markets	5.5%
2.	Anticipation of growth of markets	15.8
3.	Amicable labor relations	2.3
4.	Lower wages	7.2
5.	Availability of labor already in Florida	7.1
6.	Ease of attracting out of state personnel, incl. research	2.5
7.	Low freight cost on obtaining raw materials and components	3.8
8.	Availability of raw materials	5.7
9.	Low cost of fuel	1.1
10.	Availability of capital	1.1
11.	Low freight cost on shipping final product	10.9
12.	Adequate waste disposal possibilities	1.2
13.	Climate (as it affects operations)	11.1
14.	Community facilities	2.9
15.	State and/or municipal tax structure	2.8
16.	Climate as an attraction to top management	7.5
17.	Personal, without economic advantage	4.2
18.	Personal, with economic advantage	4.6
19.	All other factors	2.7

100.0%

Fig. 6

Percentage of Firms Citing Various Factors, Either Primarily or Secondarily, As Most Influential in Their Florida Location

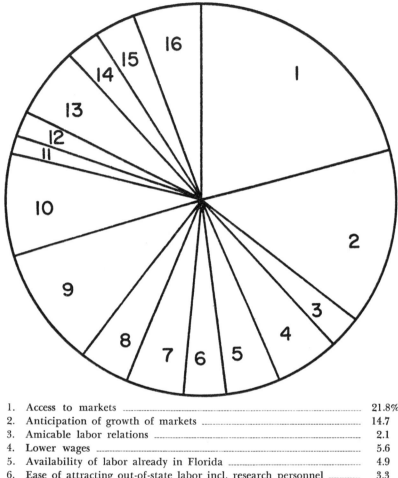

1.	Access to markets	21.8%
2.	Anticipation of growth of markets	14.7
3.	Amicable labor relations	2.1
4.	Lower wages	5.6
5.	Availability of labor already in Florida	4.9
6.	Ease of attracting out-of-state labor incl. research personnel	3.3
7.	Low freight cost on obtaining raw materials and components	5.2
8.	Availability of raw materials	3.9
9.	Low freight cost on shipping final product	10.8
10.	Climate, as it affects operations	7.8
11.	Community facilities (education, medical, police and fire)	1.9
12.	State and/or municipal tax structure	1.9
13.	Climate (as attraction to top management)	5.9
14.	Personal, with economic advantages, e.g., friendship with customers, suppliers, etc.	2.8
15.	Personal, without economic advantage	2.9
16.	All other factors	4.5

100.0%

TABLE 8.
First, Second, and Third Reasons for Location in Florida by Industry

Factor	Metal mining			Mining and quarrying of nonmetallic minerals			Construction—special trade contractors			Ordnance and accessories			Food and kindred products			Textile mill products		
	1	2	3	1	2	3	1	2	3	1	2	3	1	2	3	1	2	3
Access to markets				7						1			29	5		7		5
Anticipation of growth of markets								1			1	1	10	15			1	
Amicable labor relations																	5	
Lower wages																1	1	
Higher productivity														3	10			
Florida labor laws	1																	
Availability of labor already in Florida									5					11	8	1	1	1
Ease of attracting out-of-state skilled labor (including research personnel)										1								1
Low seller's mill price on raw materials and components											1		2					
Low freight cost on obtaining raw materials and components					1	6												
Availability of raw materials		1			6	1							19	9	2			
Low cost fuel																		
Adequate supply and satisfactory type of water																		
Availability of capital															10			
Low freight cost on shipping final product														10	22		6	
Adequate waste disposal possibilities																		
Climate (as it affects operations)															1			
Community facilities (educational, police and fire)												1			2			
Community attitudes and aid																		
State and/or municipal tax structure																5		
Climate (as an attraction to top management)							5						5					1
Personal (with economic adv. eg., friendship with customers, suppliers or bankers)							1							1	7			1
Personal (without economic adv.)														10				
TOTALS	1	1	0	7	7	7	6	5	5	2	2	2	66	64	62	14	14	9

TABLE 9.

First, Second, and Third Reasons for Location in Florida of Industry

Factor	Apparel & other finished prod. made from fabrics & similar materials			Lumber & wood prod. except furniture			Furniture and fixtures			Paper & allied products			Printing, publishing and allied prods.			Chemicals and allied products		
	1	2	3	1	2	3	1	2	3	1	2	3	1	2	3	1	2	3
Access to markets		5		25	12		17	11	1	1	6		46	36		8	2	3
Anticipation of growth of markets	1		2	10	10		6	1	25	6	5	5	11	10		1	7	6
Amicable labor relations	1							1										
Lower wages		10				16							5					
Higher productivity											1							
Florida labor laws											1	1						
Availability of labor already in Florida	10				10	3	1	5	1								1	
Ease of attracting out-of-state skilled labor (including research personnel)																		3
Low seller's mill price on raw materials and components							1										1	
Low freight cost on obtaining raw materials and components	5	2		22	5	1		1		1	1	1			5	6	2	1
Availability of raw materials				1	14	2				1		7				2	2	
Low cost fuel																		
Adequate supply and satisfactory type of water																		
Availability of capital																		
Low freight cost on shipping final product	5			14	8	18	11	1	1							7	7	2
Adequate waste disposal possibilities		6			6	5		15						5			1	
Climate (as it affects operations)																		
Community facilities (educational, police and fire)			10						1									2
Community attitudes and aid																		
State and/or municipal tax structure					5	10				5				11	5	1		
Climate (as an attraction to top management)			1			5			7						30			1
Personal (with economic adv. eg., friendship with customers, suppliers or bankers)			10				1										2	
Personal (without economic adv.)						1			1						22			
TOTALS	22	23	23	72	70	66	37	35	37	14	14	14	62	62	62	25	25	18

TABLE 10.
First, Second, and Third Reasons for Location in Florida by Industry

Industry

Factor	Petroleum refining and related products			Rubber and misc. plastic products			Leather and leather products			Stone, clay and glass products			Primary metal ind.			Fab. met. prod. except ordnance mach. & trans. equipment		
	1	2	3	1	2	3	1	2	3	1	2	3	1	2	3	1	2	3
Access to markets	11									5	1		6	5		67	5	2
Anticipation of growth of markets	1		5							34	3		5			3	26	1
Amicable labor relations																1	6	1
Lower wages				1										1		5	10	21
Higher productivity																		
Florida labor laws					1							1						
Availability of labor already in Florida		1	1															1
Ease of attracting out-of-state skilled labor (including research personnel)																5	5	
Low seller's mill price on raw materials and components																		
Low freight cost on obtaining raw materials and components										2	6						10	1
Availability of raw materials											18							
Low cost fuel																		
Adequate supply and satisfactory type of water																	1	
Availability of capital		5					15			3	1	15			6	22	7	23
Low freight cost on shipping final product																		10
Adequate waste disposal possibilities																		
Climate (as it affects operations)		6	1					15			3	20				5	28	5
Community facilities (educational, police and fire)																1		10
Community attitudes and aid										1								
State and/or municipal tax structure			5															5
Climate (as an attraction to top management)									15							1		
Personal (with economic adv. e.g., friendship with customers, suppliers or bankers)											13	1			5			5
Personal (without economic adv.)												1						2
TOTALS	12	12	12	1	1	0	15	15	15	45	45	43	11	6	11	110	98	92

TABLE 11.

First, Second, and Third Reasons for Location in Florida by Industry

Factor	Machinery, except electrical			Elec. mach. equipment and supplies			Trans-portation equipment			Instr. photo. goods, watches & clocks			Mis. mfg. industries			Motor freight trans. & warehsng.			Wholesale trade			Misc. services		
	1	2	3	1	2	3	1	2	3	1	2	3	1	2	3	1	2	3	1	2	3	1	2	3
Access to markets	54	6	5	24	9	16	42	1	1	12	1		22		1	5						1	2	3
Anticipation of growth of markets	10	10	5				1	30	2								5					2	3	1
Amicable labor relations		1	1				2	8	1	1										1			1	
Lower wages	5	6	5	1	2	1																		
Higher productivity				1	10																			
Florida labor laws					1				1															
Availability of labor already in Florida		5		3	2	1	8	8	18	11	11	1		1										1
Ease of attracting out-of-state skilled labor (including research personnel)	7	5		2	4	6	9	2	1	7	1	11										4	1	
Low seller's mill price on raw materials and components									6						1									
Low freight cost on obtaining raw materials and components													1	5										
Availability of raw materials		16																				1		
Low cost fuel			15																					
Adequate supply and satisfactory type of water																								
Availability of capital		1			5																			
Low freight cost on shipping final product	1			1		1	2	2	4					1	15			5						1
Adequate waste disposal possibilities															5									
Climate (as it affects operations)	5	20		1			2	4	12			1		1										
Community facilities (educational, police and fire)						3						1			1				1				1	
Community attitudes and aid		1				1																		
State and/or municipal tax structure			11						1															
Climate (as an attraction to top management)		10	6			3		8			1										1			1
Personal (with economic adv. eg., friendship with customers, suppliers or bankers)		1	6					2																1
Personal (without economic adv.)						1																		
TOTALS	82	77	54	34	34	34	58	57	57	20	20	14	23	23	23	5	5	5	1	1	1	7	6	3

"Amicable labor relations" was cited 11 times as the factor of first importance and 10 times as the second most significant matter in this industry. It appears that labor relations is a consideration of more concern in the printing and publishing industry than in most industries which were surveyed.

Climate as an advantage to top management was cited 30 times as the third most important factor by owners or managers of printing shops. Since a market exists for printing and publishing throughout the country, the Florida climate often appeared as the decisive factor in guiding plants to the State.

(B) Fabricated metal products plants place heavy stress on locating to gain access to markets and to secure low freight cost on shipping final products. The former determinant was cited 67 times as the primary factor and the latter 22 times. These plants are located mainly in the population centers, often producing items which enter into construction.

Significant advantage is gained by companies in this general field of activity which locate in or near the population centers. Both the Aetna Steel Company and the Florida Steel Corporation of Jacksonville stressed the advantage gained by being near selected customers. Proper servicing of a job is possible only under conditions of proximity; otherwise a local sales-engineering office would be in order if a substitute arrangement were desired. For small specialty companies that cannot afford to maintain extra offices, it becomes vital, if not imperative, to be located at places where close contact with a sufficient number of buyers is possible. Under the belief that the market in Florida offers greater demand than alternative and otherwise equivalent buying areas, a double market influence appears. We find that desire to have access to Florida markets brings the firm to Florida; in turn, the need for proximity then induces the firm to locate in a specific locality.

(C) The chemical industry shows heavy reliance on locating in such a way as to secure low freight cost on obtaining raw materials. Nevertheless, low freight cost on shipping the final product is also significant, and some branch plants which have located in Florida rather than in the Gulf states farther to the west have done so in order to be closer to the Eastern markets. Their location is an interesting compromise between getting low cost on material deliveries and low cost on shipping final products. "Access to markets" was mentioned as of first importance quite often, but scrutiny of individual returns shows that this factor is more important for chemical warehouses and packaging plants—which are located near local markets—than for the typical chemical manufacturer. (See Chapter III for detailed explanation of the difference between transport cost on the finished product and the market factor.)

(D) Furniture and fixtures manufacturing seeks access to markets and low freight cost on shipping the final product. Climate, at is affects operations, shows up as an important secondary factor. Lower manufacturing costs are possible in Florida because many items can be produced in relatively low cost factory buildings which normally require no heat. Outdoor work is also more feasible than in other states, and the sunshine is helpful in drying paint.

Successful operation in this industry requires either that the market be large or, if it is small, that rivals be few. This factor is especially vital in view of the relatively durable nature of the final product, the resulting irregular demand by any one set of buyers, the rather high freight cost involved in transporting the finished products and the resulting restricted radius over which a small manufacturer may sell. That both access to markets and low freight cost on shipping the final product appear as vital location factors in this industry is no surprise at all.

(E) Lumber and wood products other than furniture are often made near the raw material source. Access to markets was cited slightly more often as the primary factor, however, since the category covers a good number of products, such as roof trusses, which are used in construction.

Ease of Attracting Skilled Labor

Some interesting information can be obtained by examining Tables 8, 9, 10 and 11 horizontally rather than vertically. For example, "ease of attracting out-of-state skilled labor" is unimportant in many industries. It is a significant factor, however, in the production of transportation equipment (trailers, boats, etc.), instruments and machinery.

Notwithstanding the general findings noted above, there are selected industries which are greatly influenced by this factor. The Martin Company and the Sperry Electronic Tube Division of Sperry Rand, among others, were influenced greatly by considerations of this kind.

The Martin Company selected Orlando, Florida, as the home of its new division in 1956. The Division was organized to handle development and production of missiles and electronic systems under contract from the defense establishment. The Division now (1961) employs 10,000 persons and is the State's largest industrial firm.

The Orlando Division, incidentally, is the second of Martin's divisions to be set up away from Baltimore. The first, near Denver, Colorado, is engaged in the production and development of the Titan missile. The Colorado mountain area site was selected because the type of operations to be performed there—including static firings of missiles—requires a certain amount of seclusion.

The Orlando Division, on the other hand, has as its primary requisite a location which would attract an adequate supply of skilled personnel and provide space for plant expansion. The company conducted a nationwide survey to determine the regional location of this plant. The prime purpose of the survey was to determine where engineers and research personnel preferred to work. The results indicated that approximately 60 per cent of the persons surveyed preferred Florida. Accordingly, company officials were relatively sure that an adequate supply of the required type of personnel would be available in this State. The actual location in the city of Orlando was due to other special considerations, particularly community attitudes, and is a matter which takes us beyond our present interest and will be ignored.

The attraction of the Florida climate for skilled engineers and scientific personnel—an important element in the applied research function of the Sperry Electronic Tube Division of the Sperry Rand Corporation—is considered a decided asset by the Division's leadership. In 1961 the plant employed 600 persons with a staff of 1,100 planned for the future. Research and products of the Gainesville plant are taking many forms, including electronic food sterilization, microwave relay links, linear accelerators, radar apparatus, and airport landing and take-off equipment.

Plant management has found that the attitude of local employees has brought high productivity to the operation. A willingness to direct their efforts toward the opportunities for more technical training leading to more complex jobs has been manifest.

The mild climate is also credited with reducing operating costs in many cases through a variety of plant and personnel advantages, and is cited as a dominant factor behind Sperry's decision to locate in Florida.

Personal Factors with Economic Advantages

Personal factors with economic advantages due to friendship with customers, suppliers, bankers, and others do not rank high in most fields. They appear to be significant, however, in the manufacture of apparel, stone, clay, and glass products. Where relevant, these considerations serve to induce a businessman to stay near his hometown.

Wage Rates

Relatively low wage rates do not show up very often as a factor attracting plants. In part this seems to be due to a reluctance to cite this factor on a questionnaire since it is mentioned quite often in the course of personal interviews. Where labor is in abundant supply relative to demand, which is especially the situation in rural counties and in communities with many retired but still competent workers, the low wage rates in relation to productivity can be an important factor in making a business venture feasible. Lower wages as a factor among the first three in importance show up most often in the manufacture of food and kindred products, apparel, lumber and wood products, fabricated metal products, machinery, and transportation equipment. A substantial number of companies stressed the need for competitive wages, for an adequate supply of workers, for low labor turnover and, in general, their desire to have amicable labor relations. To many of these firms, amicable labor relations was synonymous with the non-existence of labor unions.[1]

Community Factors

Officials of new plants were asked not only to check and rank the factors which caused them to locate in Florida but also to state what factor or factors caused them to select a particular city. Answers to this question are often the same as for the State in general.

---

[1]The attraction of a relatively low wage area to new plants and the amount of employment afforded by existing plants can both be affected adversely by minimum wage legislation. See M. R. Colberg, "Minimum Wage Effects on Florida's Economic Development," *Journal of Law and Economics,* October, 1960, pp. 106-117.

TABLE 12.

First, Second, and Third Reasons for Location in Community by Industry

Factor	Metal mining			Mining and quarrying of nonmetallic minerals			Construction—special trade contractors			Ordnance and accessories			Food and kindred products			Textile mill products		
	1	2	3	1	2	3	1	2	3	1	2	3	1	2	3	1	2	3
Access to markets										1			17			5		
Anticipation of growth of markets																	1	
Amicable labor relations																		
Lower wages								1			2	1		2	1			
Higher productivity																		
Florida labor laws																		
Availability of labor already in Florida													2	1		2		
Ease of attracting out-of-state skilled labor (including research personnel)										1						1		
Low seller's mill price on raw materials and components															1			
Low freight cost on obtaining raw materials and components	1												5	2	1			
Availability of raw materials				7									2	2				
Low cost fuel																		
Low cost of elec. power																		
Adequate supply and satisfactory type of water														3				
Low cost of capital																		
Availability of capital													1					
Low freight cost on shipping final product													16	10	2			
Adequate waste disposal possibilities															2			
Climate (as it affects operations)																		
Community facilities (educational, police and fire)											1		7	6	2			
Community attitudes and aid														7	7	6		
State and/or municipal tax structure												1						
Climate (as an attraction to top management)																		
Personal (with economic adv. eg., friendship with customers, suppliers or bankers)							5						1					
Personal (without economic adv.)							1											
TOTALS	1			7			6	1		2	3	2	51	33	16	14	1	

TABLE 13.
First, Second, and Third Reasons for Location in Community by Industry

Factor	Apparel & other finished prod. made from fabrics & similar materials			Lumber & wood products furniture			Furniture and fixtures			Paper & allied products			Printing, publishing and allied prods.			Chemicals and allied products		
	1	2	3	1	2	3	1	2	3	1	2	3	1	2	3	1	2	3
Access to markets				8	6		17	11		7			46			7		
Anticipation of growth of markets	10						1							30		1		
Amicable labor relations																		
Lower wages																		
Higher productivity																		
Florida labor laws							5		10		1							
Availability of labor already in Florida		1																
Ease of attracting out-of-state skilled labor (including research personnel)																		
Low seller's mill price on raw materials and components				2														
Low freight cost on obtaining raw materials and components		2		25	1					1				5		3	2	
Availability of raw materials						1				1	6					1	2	
Low cost fuel																		
Low cost of elec. power																1		
Adequate supply and satisfactory type of water											1					2		1
Low cost of capital																		
Availability of capital																	1	
Low freight cost on shipping final product				12	2	1	10					1					5	1
Adequate waste disposal possibilities												1					1	
Climate (as it affects operations)																		
Community facilities (educational, police and fire)	10			10	4	1	1			5			1				1	
Community attitudes and aid	3				5	2							5				3	1
State and/or municipal tax structure							1											
Climate (as an attraction to top management)				5			1								5	5		
Personal (with economic adv. eg., friendship with customers, suppliers or bankers)				10													1	
Personal (without economic adv.)			1										10	1				
TOTALS	23	3	1	72	18	5	36	11	10	14	8	2	62	36	5	23	13	2

TABLE 14.

First, Second, and Third Reasons for Location in Community by Industry

Factor	Petroleum refining and related products			Rubber and misc. plastic products			Leather and leather products			Stone, clay and glass products			Primary metal ind.			Fab. met. prod. except ordnance mach. & trans. equipment		
	1	2	3	1	2	3	1	2	3	1	2	3	1	2	3	1	2	3
Access to markets		5								9						71		
Anticipation of growth of markets	2		5							19	1		6			6	6	
Amicable labor relations				1														
Lower wages																		
Higher productivity																		
Florida labor laws																		
Availability of labor already in Florida					1											1		
Ease of attracting out-of-state skilled labor (including research personnel)																		
Low seller's mill price on raw materials and components																	20	
Low freight cost on obtaining raw materials and components							15				2	1				5		
Availability of raw materials	5																	
Low cost fuel																		
Low cost of elec. power																		
Adequate supply and satisfactory type of water																		
Low cost of capital																		
Availability of capital																		
Low freight cost on shipping final product										2	1					2	1	
Adequate waste disposal possibilities																		
Climate (as it affects operations)																		
Community facilities (educational, police and fire)										2	1					17	1	
Community attitudes and aid						1				1								1
State and/or municipal tax structure																5		
Climate (as an attraction to top management)	5									12			5					
Personal (with economic adv. eg., friendship with customers, suppliers or bankers)																1		1
Personal (without economic adv.)																1		20
TOTALS	12	5	5	1	1	1	15			45	5	1	11			109	28	22

TABLE 15.

First, Second, and Third Reasons for Location in Community by Industry

Factor	Machinery, except electrical			Elec. mach. equipment and supplies			Transportation equipment			Instr. photo. goods, watches & clocks			Mis. mfg. industries			Motor freight trans. & warehsng.			Wholesale trade			Misc. services		
	1	2	3	1	2	3	1	2	3	1	2	3	1	2	3	1	2	3	1	2	3	1	2	3
Access to markets	43	5		12	1		31	4		12			21			5						2	1	2
Anticipation of growth of markets								10	1															
Amicable labor relations																								
Lower wages					10	10	6	1																
Higher productivity																								
Florida labor laws																								
Availability of labor already in Florida			10	3	1		1	15	7			10												
Ease of attracting out-of-state skilled labor (including research personnel)				2			7				1	1												
Low seller's mill price on raw materials and components													1									1		
Low freight cost on obtaining raw materials and components		5							1											1				
Availability of raw materials		16																						
Low cost fuel																								
Low cost of elec. power																								
Adequate supply and satisfactory type of water																								
Low cost of capital							3																	
Availability of capital	1	2			5			1																
Low freight cost on shipping final product						1	3	1			1												1	
Adequate waste disposal possibilities																								
Climate (as it affects operations)	5					1																		
Community facilities (educational, police and fire)	17	5	5	12	8	5	5	7	1	2	1								1			4		
Community attitudes and aid			5				1	1	1		11													
State and/or municipal tax structure				3				2																
Climate (as an attraction to top management)		5			2	5			26															
Personal (with economic adv. eg., friendship with customers, suppliers or bankers)	6	6	17	2	2																			
Personal (without economic adv.)	5	5	1			1				6														
TOTALS	77	49	38	34	29	23	57	42	37	20	14	11	22			5			1	1		7	2	2

The question tends to bring out factors which vary a good deal from one community to another.

Personal factors with economic advantages are cited often as guiding a firm to a particular locality, as may be seen in Tables 12, 13, 14, and 15. Community facilities for education, medical care, police and fire protection are frequently named. Availability of labor in the community shows up often. Access to market appears regularly since the market is sometimes restricted to a single community and since cities can differ markedly as market centers. Quite vital in many cases was the attitude of civic leaders toward industrial development. The Tiffany Tile Corporation of Port Tampa was among those influenced favorably by community attitudes. The Martin Company selected its particular Florida location in part because it found the amount of land it needed readily available. The friendly attitude of bankers, civic leaders, and average citizens proved to be the extra inducement which caused the company to select Orlando.

Summary

Access to markets, ease of attracting skilled workers, relatively low wages, climate, and community facilities are but a few of the many factors that influenced the location of the diverse kinds of plants and industries which recently located in Florida. Reference to the tables and figures in this chapter will uncover data of special and even more restricted nature than most of those that were described above. Through such examination further insight and details can be obtained concerning the forces which have led new plants to selected localities in the State.

CHAPTER VI

LOCATION FACTORS IN URBAN AND RURAL COUNTIES

Introduction

For some time now industrial development commissions have been in vogue in the United States. These units frequently are formed under state auspices; sometimes the county or municipality charters the agency; occasionally direction is given by private capital. The purpose of the group in practically every case is to develop an area economically, with greatest emphasis usually being placed on attracting manufacturing and mining establishments and less often on bringing in wholesaling and financial activity. A basic part of the development commission program is to understand the resources of the area in question. Comparable interest attaches to the matter of which industries can be attracted by the resources that exist in the area in question.

The need for correlating resources with industrial location factors has its counterpart in so-called "location" and "industry" studies. These studies tend to take two forms. First must come the broad location study which is designed to cover the whole field, like the one described in the previous pages. Examination of the location factors that played a role in causing different industries to locate in the area in question provides certain insight which can be utilized in the future. Indeed, if the study is well conceived and executed, a rather full picture can be gained about location forces in general for the several types of industry which conceivably might be attracted in greater and greater numbers to the region under examination.

As a sub-part of the general location study itself, there should be an analysis which describes existing industrial patterns, discusses desirable patterns, and accounts for the ways that the two can be mixed in forthcoming years. This inquiry stresses the types of industry which the commission considers to be the "kind of activity desired for the area," *and* if the general location study points to the feasibility of attracting this kind of industry to the area, then the development officials may be well on their way to attaining their objective.

There remains the second and last main stage of development commission economic research: the effecting of special industrial studies as indicated by the initial research activity. These special industrial studies must cover a range of matters extending from the location of material sources, the transportation conditions in the industry, the labor types needed, other processing cost matters, and finally the price policies and type of competition that prevails in the industry. Only after such detailed study is completed will the "sales-pitch" men be able to work effectively. Manifestly, the commission which really influences plant location is the one that does not strive for over-night accomplishments but rather bides its time in careful evaluation of its own area. We propose that this requires a study of general location principles in the subject area, including industry types desired, and then a detailed study of selected industries.

It is the general purpose of this chapter to examine one small phase of the whole complex matter of general *industrial development* economic research, namely, the analyzing of data acquired through a general location study of Florida. We do not review the weighty issue of how to set up a location study which complies with theoretical constructs nor the inherent problem of how to mold a system of understandable questions. Rather, we let previous chapters suffice and note here only that if the theoretical support is lacking, the survey itself must be lacking, and any attempt to analyze its data must be misleading.[1]

We omit also in the present chapter further mention of the related problems of selecting the activity types that are most needed by the area in question and which would best fit the economy of that area.[2] We place ourselves in the position of the officials of underdeveloped counties in Florida imagining how they might use the data described herein for the purpose of broadening the industrial base of their counties.

Selected Statistical Findings

(A)   Industries Preferring Certain Types of Counties

It was found that the food and kindred products industry (SIC 20), the lumber and wood products industry (SIC 24), and the

---

[1]See M. L. Greenhut's "An Empirical Model And A Survey," *Review of Economics and Statistics*, XLI, (1959), 433-438.

[2]This aspect of the general problem area is discussed in detail in Chapters 3 and 8 of a private report by M. L. Greenhut on *The Economy of Valdosta and its Industrial Potential*, submitted to the Industrial Development Branch, The Georgia Institute of Technology, 1959.

chemical industry (SIC 28) located relatively willingly in what are designated the "underdeveloped" counties in Florida. In contrast, the publishing and printing industry (SIC 27), the fabricated metal products industry (SIC 34), and the electrical machinery industry (SIC 36) clearly preferred locations in the developed counties.

The industries cited above which proved most willing to locate in underdeveloped counties preferred this kind of location only relatively rather than absolutely, and then in some cases only for certain sizes of plants. But first recall, from Chapter V, that considering all industries, and taking those firms with less than 25 employees, a preference rate existed for developed counties slightly greater than 7-1, while for firms of all sizes the ratio was less than 6-1, being especially low in the 25-99 and 100-499 employee category. (See Table 1.) In related manner, the less-than-25 employee firms in the food and kindred products industry preferred developed counties at a ratio of about 12-1, with, however, the relative preference for location in developed counties changing as larger establishments are considered, falling to slightly more than 3-1 as all firms in the industry are considered.[3] (See Table 1 for ratios and Table 2 for numerical details.)

Similar figures prevail in lumber and wood products. There the firms in the less-than-25 employees classification preferred the developed counties at approximately a 2-1 figure. Underdeveloped and developed counties were selected on an equal basis by firms in the 25-99 employee group. And because companies in this industry were all below the 100 employee classification, our total ratio figure reflects such small scale plants and leaves a relative preference for developed counties over underdeveloped counties of about 1½-1. (See Tables 1 and 2.)

The chemical industry shows comparable results. Among small sized plants (0-24 employees), developed counties were preferred by a ratio of 2-1. Where 25-99 employees were hired, the preference

---

[3]Incidentally, one finds throughout the statistics presented here (except for the largest size plants, *i.e.*, more than 500 employees), a surprisingly greater willingness among the larger employee establishments to locate in underdeveloped counties. While readers may have anticipated a preference among the bigger plants for location where large numbers of people live and hence where many workers are available, apparently the relatively large size establishment believes that it can tap a "labor market" in underdeveloped counties to greater advantage and have little difficulty in inducing workers to commute the necessary distances.

TABLE 1.

Approximate Preference Ratios Among Surveyed Plants for Developed County Locations Compared to Underdeveloped Counties, in Selected Industries and in Total, 1956-57

	0-24 Employees	25-99 Employees	Employees 100-499	500 Employees and over	All Employee Groups
Food & Kindred Products	12-1	1-7	1-1	1-0	3½-1
Lumber & Wood Products	2-1	1-1	0-0	0-0	1½-1
Chemicals	2-1	2-3	0-4	1-0	1-1
Electrical Machinery	20-0	2-0	4-1	2-0	16-1
Printing	30-1	0-0	0-0	0-0	30-1
Fabricated Metal Products	13-1	12-0	6-0	0-0	16-1
All Industries	7-1	3-1	3-1	8-1	6-1

rate was 2-3; that is, underdeveloped counties were actually preferred. For firms with more than 100 employees, the underdeveloped counties again were preferred with the ratio of urban to rural being 1 to 4.

Significant contrast is shown by the industry groups which most preferred location in developed counties. Among these, the electrical machinery plants with less than 25 employees preferred the developed counties at a 20-0 figure. Among the 25-99 employee plants in this industry, the preference amounted to 2-0, while an 8-2 absolute preference or 4-1 ratio prevailed for plants having more than 100 and less than 500 employees. Above this employee total, the preference was 2-0. The overall total showed 32-2 firms preferring developed counties or a 16-1 ratio in the industry.

All new firms in Florida in the printing industry had less than 25 employees. Total figures for the industry are therefore equal to the small plant industry figures. The preference rate was 30-1— a striking preference for urban locations.

Firms in the fabricated metal products industry employing less than 25 workers preferred the developed counties at an 80-6 figure or a rate approximating 13-1. Among firms with employees between 25 and 99 in number, the preference value was 12-0; and similarly 6 to 0 for establishments with between 100 and 499 employees which formed the largest size firms in this industrial group. The preference rate, in total, ran more than 16-1 for location in developed counties in this industry. Table 2 shows the actual numbers of plants on which the ratios are based.

TABLE 2.
Location of Surveyed Plants by Size, and Type of County, 1956-57

County Type	Plant Size (Employees)	Industry Group							
		Food & Kindred Products	Lumber & Wood Prod.	Chemicals	Electrical Machinery	Printing	Fab. Metal Products	All Other Industries	All Industries
Developed	0-24	47	40	10	20	60	80	268	525
	25-99	1	5	2	2	0	12	47	69
	100-499	3	0	0	8	0	6	23	40
	500-over	1	0	1	2	0	0	4	8
	Sub Total	52	45	13	32	60	98	342	642
Underdeveloped	0-24	4	22	5	0	2	6	31	70
	25-99	7	5	3	2	0	0	11	26
	100-499	3	0	4	2	0	0	4	13
	500-over	0	0	0	0	0	0	1	1
	Sub Total	14	27	12	2	2	6	47	110
	Total	66	72	25	34	62	104	389	752

Certain Generalizations

We may distill from these figures, albeit with some caution,[4] the following generalizations. Underdeveloped counties in Florida and generally in similar states have the greatest natural chance of attracting plants in the food and kindred products industry, in the lumber and wood products industry, and in the chemicals industry. Because plants with less than 25 employees do not represent a very significant gain for a county, those counties with limited resources for financing development programs probably should exert particular effort to attract the chemicals and food and kindred product industries, where plants are often relatively large. This effort would tend to attach secondary importance to the small plants in food and kindred products, in lumber and wood products, and in the chemicals industries, letting them ferret out the county in question chiefly by natural process, *i.e.,* original inquiry being made by the firm itself without active solicitation by county developers.

The chemical industry suggests an exciting potential for the officials of underdeveloped counties, especially if a significant size location is desired. It is in this industry that fairly large plants (100-499 employees) appear to have strongest preference for location in underdeveloped counties; at least this is true on the basis of the Florida study. Study of the location factors influencing plant location in this industry, examination of preferences for location sites, cross-check of transport conditions, raw material sources, markets and prices, and finally of existing regional and state locations in the industry should provide county officials with the information necessary to help them persuade would-be locators to establish plants in the specific county. This assumes, of course, that on the basis of the information acquired, the location would prove economic and that "social costs" in the form of smoke, waste products, *etc.,* are not excessive.

An alternative to attracting a new chemical plant might be to gain "wholesaling" facilities under a manufacturer's sales-representative contract. Interesting as this possibility may be, it is clearly a smaller success than the attracting of an actual manufacturing

---

[4]Whether the inductive leaps which follow trap us into error, especially with respect to states in different areas and regions, will be determined ultimately by comparisons with other studies.

plant. In any case, contact established for a plant may lead to sales representative contracts, if nothing else.

(B) Further Analysis of Survey Statistics: State Location Factor Differences among the Industries in Question

(1) The firms comprising the food and kindred products industry and preferring location in developed counties differed substantially in their location factor selection from those firms locating in underdeveloped counties. Size of plant, as shown in Table 3, made little difference in this respect. Thirty-eight companies of the fifty-two locating in developed counties selected the demand factors (access to markets or anticipating the growth of markets) as the main determinant. Five were influenced primarily by climate, seven by low freight cost on raw materials, and one each by low mill price on raw materials and availability of raw materials. Approximately three out of four in this industry preferring location in developed counties were highly influenced by market factors. In contrast, twelve out of fourteen locating in underdeveloped counties did so to gain low freight cost on raw materials. This 6-1 ratio suggests the kind of sales appeals which officials in underdeveloped counties must use, namely, an approach which stresses that raw materials are more expensive to transport than finished products and that by location near a source of materials the firm will cut its costs and be able to produce a special product. Through this cost saving, food and kindred products firms may sell in markets at more favorable prices than firms that fail to gain this advantage.

On taking a closer look than is afforded by Table 3 we have noted that the meat packing plants (3-0), the sea food canneries (2-0), and the fruit canneries (2-0) were ready locators in underdeveloped counties. On the other hand, the companies in the food and kindred products industry which located predominantly in the developed counties were those which fall into the malt liquor and other beverages group (13 companies to 0) and prepared feeds (20-1).

Each of the meat packers claimed that low freight costs on obtaining raw materials governed its particular location decisions. Those packaging sea foods were also primarily concerned with the same consideration, as were the fruit canneries.

The malt liquor beverage group was similarly unanimous in

TABLE 3.

First Locational Factor Selected by Selected Industries by Number of Employees and County Type

Factors	0-24 Dev.	0-24 UD	25-99 Dev.	25-99 UD	100-499 Dev.	100-499 UD	500-over Dev.	500-over UD	All Sizes Dev.	All Sizes UD	Factor Totals
FOOD AND KINDRED PRODUCTS											
Access to markets	27	1	1						28	1	29
Anticipation of growth of market	10								10	0	10
Low sellers mill price on raw material					1				1	1	2
Low freight cost to obtain raw material	5	2		7	1	3	1		7	12	19
Availability of raw material					1				1	0	1
Climate as attraction to top management	5								5		5
LUMBER AND WOOD PRODUCTS EXCEPT FURNITURE											
Access to markets	15	4	5	1					20	5	25
Anticipation of growth of market	10								10	0	10
Low freight cost to obtain raw material	5	13		4					5	17	22
Availability of raw material		1							0	1	1
Low freight cost on shipping final product	10	4							10	4	14
CHEMICALS AND ALLIED PRODUCTS											
Access to markets	5	2	1						6	2	8
Anticipation of growth of market		1							0	1	1
Ease of attracting out-of-state skilled labor	1		1						1	0	1
Low freight cost to obtain raw material	1			2		2	1		1	5	6
Availability of raw material				1		2			0	2	2
Low freight cost on shipping final product	5	1				1			5	2	7

selecting their dominant factor. However, with this group, access to markets governed the site selection. Apparently by selecting developed counties for location, this kind of concern enhanced its profit making ability. Similarly, the prepared feeds group appeared equally concerned with market potential, and on a near unanimous basis selected this factor as the dominant force behind its locations. Lone dissent comes from the one member of this industry that located in an underdeveloped county. We see in this last case that low freight on raw material was dominating.

Let us draw the following conservative conclusions from these observations. Canneries and other packagers of foods (including meat, sea food, and fruits) tend to locate near raw materials. They are not concerned with the stage of county development, being in fact very willing to locate in underdeveloped places. Breweries and prepared foods manufacturers, on the other hand, concentrate heavily on developed counties, though millers of grain other than foods move readily to underdeveloped counties.[5] Fruit processors were found in either type of county; their major interest in minimizing freight cost on raw materials and hence in locating wherever the materials are found is not surprising.

(2) The lumber and wood products (except furniture) industry exhibits similar contrasts. Thirty of the companies preferring developed county locations were market influenced firms. Ten wanted low freight cost on the final product, and five sought low freight cost on raw materials. In ratio form, the preference was 2-1 for the demand (*i.e.,* market) factor among the firms in developed counties, presumably with proximity to buyers being a basic component of the factor. On the other hand, seventeen of the lumber and wood product enterprises locating in underdeveloped counties sought low freight cost on raw materials. Five wanted access to markets, four sought low freight cost on the final product, and one wanted to gain a ready supply of raw materials. The preference rate among these firms was little less than 2-1 for the saving of cost on shipping raw materials over all other main considerations.

On the basis of these statistics it appears that officials in underdeveloped counties should usually stress the raw material transport

---

[5]Significantly three of the four "small' concerns selecting underdeveloped counties were in the grain mill products classification.

cost advantage accruing to lumber and wood product operations in their counties.

On levels of analysis more detailed than is provided in Table 3, certain clear-cut relationships appear. Nineteen logging camps located in under-developed counties and only five in developed counties. Two of the companies locating in underdeveloped counties claimed that access to markets brought them to Florida; three were most concerned with low freight cost on their finished product and significantly confined their product sales to Florida. The fourteen others, along with all those locating in developed counties, sought to minimize freight costs on raw materials. The saw mill and planing mill group (three in number) all located in underdeveloped counties, while oppositely the millwork group, including prefabricated wooden structures, such as buildings, sections, and panels, confined their locations to developed counties.

Loggers, planing mills and sawmills locate where forests exist and usually these are found in underdeveloped areas. The business organizations in this category are usually small in size and seek to minimize the freight costs on raw materials. Their mills fabricate either rough, round, *hewn or river primary* forest or wood raw materials, and they locate these mills or their sawing and planing operations as near to the center of the raw material supply as is possible. Either the county developer has the forests or he does not. Even if he does, his area may need a market or cost advantage over other areas in order to gain these types of fabricating facilities.

At the more advanced stages of production, such as millwork and prefabricated processing, a clear tendency exists to locate in developed counties. The lure of markets strongly influenced the location of millworks in Florida, while low freight costs on final products tended to dominate the location of prefabricated wooden construction firms. For the officials of underdeveloped counties, one must conclude that economic forces leave little leeway. Perhaps the miscellaneous wood products group (including such items as particle board, cork products, mirror and picture frames) which located in the developed counties of Florida, might yet be convinced that underdeveloped county location is feasible. But certainly, the need for preliminary studies is indicated before a strong enough sales pitch can be offered, for at least the statistics of 1956-57 locations in Florida suggest a tendency to orient toward the more developed counties.

(3) The chemical and allied products group is the last industry covered by Table 3. Among the thirteen firms in this industry selecting developed counties, six considered access to markets to be *the* location factor. Five of these chemical firms were influenced primarily by the desire to minimize shipping costs on the final product. This particular consideration suggests that for these firms the industrial process involves the addition of weight, bulk, or perishability so that shipping the final product over shortest distances reduces costs. One of these chemical concerns wanted a location that would best attract out-of-state labor, and the other sought lowest freight costs on raw materials. To repeat, six of the thirteen that located in developed counties did so because of access to markets.

In sharp contrast, five of the chemical firms locating in underdeveloped counties wanted to minimize freight costs on the raw materials, two sought a ready supply of raw materials in selecting their location, two wanted to minimize freight costs on shipping the final product, and three were market influenced. Again, we suggest that officials of underdeveloped counties would do well to emphasize freight cost advantages on raw materials when trying to induce chemical companies to locate in their county. This emphasis does not mean that such factors as waste disposal facilities can be ignored. It means simply that the greatest variable in the industry is often the transportation costs on raw materials. Presumably, there are many places offering or able to offer adequate waste disposal facilities, but only selected places which yield low freight cost on the raw materials because of ideal county location, *i.e.,* advantageous material to market relationships.

Examination of particular activity types in detail beyond that of Table 3 uncovers a pronounced tendency for those companies engaged in the manufacture of detergents and cleaning preparations (ten in number) to locate in developed counties. For these companies, size of markets, including proximity to buyers (or low freight cost on the finished product is more important. Significantly, these companies are small in size tending to employ around 25 workers or less. Their markets are sometimes the southeastern United States but the prevailing market is in Florida. These industries, because their markets are primarily local in nature, tend to move into urban counties which provide them with these local markets.

Other activity types that selected developed counties include a firm manufacturing industrial gases, a producer of fertilizers, and a company manufacturing synthetic organic fibers. Each of these organizations was large in size, employing more than 100 workers. Respectively, they were influenced by the desire to attract skilled labor, by the market, and by low freight cost on raw materials. But each of these company types may also be found in the underdeveloped counties. There we find that an industrial gas company was concerned most with minimizing freight cost on the final product, while the fertilizer and synthetics unit agreed with their developed county counterparts in selecting respectively the Florida agricultural market and low freight cost on raw materials as the prime location variable.

Examination of the list of companies locating in underdeveloped counties revealed a wide distribution of activity types. These companies ranged from a producer of agricultural pesticides to gum and wood chemical plants, to a paints and lacquer establishment[6] and to industrial organic chemical concerns. Availability of raw materials was primary to two of three gum and wood chemical concerns, while low freight cost on raw materials was considered most important by the other firm. Also, the two organic chemical companies that located in underdeveloped counties in Florida were most influenced by this factor of location. Certainly, the experiences in Florida in recent years suggest that this industry is quite willing to locate in underdeveloped counties. Frequently the companies were large and only the small concerns appeared weighted in favor of developed counties.

------

[6]It is noteworthy that the paint, varnish and lacquer industry is a prime prospect for most commissions. One may readily understand this since there are over 1500 plants of this kind in the nation, with the dispersion of plants being fairly general. (And see the U.S. Dept. of Commerce, 15 Leading Paint Producing States, *1954 Census of Manufactures,* pp. 284-285.) Study, for example, of paint plants in the South would show that most of them are small, produce rather specialized products appealing to selected industries or particular consumer use, and are spread evenly over space in such manner that, for any given product and price, the production tends to be found in the largest city of its market area. Within this market area, the subject firm is alone or dominant. It follows that if the demand for the product happens to be so scattered in space that the existence of one plant, wherever it is located, leaves room for another plant, the optimum location of this plant may as readily as not fall in a generally underdeveloped county.

(C) Supplementary Factors and Other Industries

Extension of the study to secondary and tertiary factors, if done chiefly in terms of the food and kindred products industry, the lumber and wood products industry, and the chemical industry, uncovers certain additional information which warrants mention. For example, the food and kindred products industry showed that adequate supply of low wage labor, availability of low cost capital, and favorable community facilities and attitudes were major considerations. In turn, the lumber and wood products men stressed the need for a steadily available supply of raw materials and of relatively low wage labor as factors of major consideration in selecting their location. Chemical industry locators were interested in the ease of attracting out-of-state labor and are strongly concerned with waste disposal facilities and community attitudes and facilities in general.

We turn now to a new group of industries which, on the basis of the Florida survey, show some inclination to locate in the economically underdeveloped areas (albeit not so strong a willingness as the food and kindred products group, the chemical or lumber-wood products industry) and to other industries which, for special reasons, appear to be approachable by officials of underdeveloped counties. We will find here that the transportation equipment and the stone, clay, and glass industries were governed by factors similar to those which caused, say, the chemical industry to locate readily in the underdeveloped areas of Florida. Next, we will examine those industries which seemingly require developed county locations.

(D) The Transportation Equipment and Stone, Clay, and Glass Industries

In the transportation equipment industry, forty-three firms sought access to markets, existing or potential, as the primary factor. Two of the companies (both in aircraft) sold over a national market with the Florida location serving to increase the demand for the product in the sense that a great part of the buying activity takes place in Florida as if the market were concentrated there. Twenty-six of the other firms sold only in Florida, while an additional seven sold in the Southeast with emphasis on Florida. All of these firms just enumerated located in developed counties. (See Table 4.)

TABLE 4.

The Transportation Equipment Industry: Primary Factors in Location

	Developed County Location	Underdeveloped County Location	Total
Markets (access and growth)	35	8	43
Ease of attracting skilled labor	9	0	9
Other factors (*e.g.,* low wages, climate as it affects operations)	2	4	6
Total number of firms	46	12	58

Eight firms in the transportation equipment industry located in underdeveloped counties but claimed the same "access to market" factor as being most important. Among these, five included other southeastern states in their market area, while three sold only in Florida. One of the three was in aircraft and situated near an air force base, one was a boatbuilding concern located on the Gulf at what could be called a center of boating activity, and the other, a trailer coach manufacturer, was rather centrally located in the State.

Fifteen concerns in this transportation equipment industry stress primary factors other than markets. Eleven of this group located in developed counties and four in underdeveloped counties. Ease of attracting skilled labor was mentioned nine times in all, low wages two times, as were climate as it affects operations and low cost on shipping the final product.

Special interest attaches to the four concerns that were attracted to underdeveloped areas. In this category, we find that two were in boat building and the others in aircraft. Low labor cost was, in general, their leading factor. By extending the list to include secondary and tertiary forces as well as factors which drew the company to its particular community, we find in a prominent position the importance of gaining a site where adequate supplies of labor exist and where community facilities are favorable.

One might conclude that the underdeveloped counties have a chance of attracting the manufacturers of transportation equipment when special conditions or resources exist which can be used as a means for demonstrating the equipment. Labor supply and cost factors appear vital to many concerns, but, most important of all, the heavy stress placed on the market factor suggests that though sales may even be national, a buying pattern prevails in many parts of this industry which finds expression in the willingness of buyers to travel to the seller's plant for purposes of shopping around and then ordering their equipment. If this is so, officials in under-developed counties may search for reasons why buyers of a certain product would tend naturally to be passing through or near the county. Good highway facilities, adequate air-travel connections and their like would seem to be important. In general, the de-veloped counties tend to have a natural and strong advantage over the underdeveloped counties in these respects.

The stone, clay, and glass products industry is a rather hetero-geneous industry in which markets again dominate as the primary factor but in which availability of raw materials was significant as was the personal factor with economic advantage, *i.e.*, where the individual through background in a community has established relations which yield him an economic advantage. In fact, twelve in this group were influenced most in *selecting their community* location by personal contact advantages. Apparently if one is brought up in an environment that provides him with background experience and acquaintanceships in a business in this field, he tends to stay at home in the same occupation. Clearly, this kind of information does not provide very helpful knowledge to community officials who are interested in new kinds of industrial development. That thirty-nine firms were most influenced by the market factor and sold to buyers located only in Florida is of some better use. (See Table 5.) It suggests that market areas are not extensive. Five of the thirty-nine market-influenced firms located in underdeveloped counties, and four of these five were engaged in manufacturing concrete products with the other being engaged in fabricating brick and structural clay tile. All five were small.

TABLE 5.

The Stone, Clay, and Glass Products Industry: Primary Factors in Location

	Developed County Location	Underdeveloped County Location	Total
Markets (access and growth)	34	5	39
Other factors	3	3	6
Total number of firms	37	8	45

The counterparts in developed counties were also small in most cases, although two large market-influenced firms in the developed counties were fabricating hydraulic cement, and one large plant was an asbestos products manufacturer. Among the six in the industry not dominated by the market factor, those in the underdeveloped counties (three in number) were fabricators of concrete products and were most concerned with transport costs, while a large glass container manufacturer and a floor tile fabricator were joined by a concrete products plant among the developed county firms that stressed a primary factor other than markets.

Examination of secondary and tertiary factors provides little new information. For county developers we may conclude that small concrete products plants are likely prospects for location in principal cities of underdeveloped counties which are not close to large metropolitan areas. Indeed, it is with past or present residents who have had experience in this industry that chances appear high to gain entrepreneurial expansion in stone, clay, and glass manufacture.

(E)   The Shiftable (?) Developed County Industries

There were only a few industries that concentrated in developed counties which conceivably could have been influenced to locate in underdeveloped counties. This judgment is drawn especially in light of the kind of factors which influenced their location decisions and the geographic extent of their market. Among the firms and industries locating in developed counties and not restricted by the market factor to this kind of location, there prevailed nonetheless a set of factors that in the past consistently favored the developed county. For example, of the nine counties acquiring plants in the new Florida electrical machinery industry, which usually strives for sales to buyers located outside of Florida, three were most influenced by the availability of labor in Florida. Two of the nine were influenced by the ease of attracting out-of-state skilled labor. The others were influenced by such considerations as the availability of repair facilities, which tend to be met best in the urban counties.

A study of the apparel industry shows that among fourteen companies catering to out-of-state buyers, a significant number (six) emphasized availability of labor as primary, while low freight cost on finished product was cited five times. Unfortunately for some underdeveloped counties, if low freight costs on the finished product are important, a location in populated areas might appear to be indicated more often than not.

The machinery (except electrical) industry shows fifteen cases of firms which located in developed counties but which sell to markets situated at a distance. Significantly, ten of these firms appear as types which might have located in underdeveloped counties under slightly different circumstances. Low wages governed the location of many of these plants and climate as it affects operations (not as it attracts skilled labor or top management) influenced the others that we consider to be likely prospect types. County officials interested in this industry group would do well to stress the wage level and the advantages of the local climate. Incidentally, out of the whole group of new Florida companies in this industry, twenty listed climate as it affects operations as a factor of secondary importance, which number exceeded all other second factors. Availability of raw materials followed next in importance, being mentioned sixteen times, while climate as an attraction to top management was indicated by sixteen companies as of primary or secondary importance.

Fifteen firms in the publishing and printing industry—traditional developed county locators—sold to distant markets and stressed amicable labor relations and low wages. Good labor relations appear especially important to members of this industry, and this opens a wedge for county officials who want this type of establishment and/or who have received an inquiry from this type of manufacturer.

(F)   The Nonshiftable Developed County Industries

Detailed analysis of the Florida findings suggests that underdeveloped counties would have small chance of attracting such industry types as leather and leather products, electrical machinery, and scientific instruments. To realize a better industrial structure, the underdeveloped county must work with what it has and what it probably can get. Only after it has grown in this way will it be able to broaden out to attract the other kinds of industry which would yield it the industrial complex it hopes some day to have.

(G)   The Larger Plants

While Florida, more than most states, is the home of small business, it should be kept in mind that one large plant may provide hundreds or even thousands of times as much employment and output per period as a small plant. Special attention is focused on the plants with over 25 employees in this section. Some separate data will be provided also for plants with 100 to 499 employees and for those with an even larger number of workers.

Beginning first with the last-mentioned group—the largest plants —it is evident from previous statistics that access to markets does not loom so large a factor of location as it does for smaller plants. Instead, "amicable labor relations" was cited more often than any other factor as one of the advantages of locating in Florida. This is shown in Table 6. Branch plants of large firms and large plants which relocated in Florida from other states frequently mentioned this factor.

Six other factors were cited almost as frequently by officials of the very largest plants. These were "access to markets," "lower wages," "availability of labor in Florida," "ease of attracting out-of-state skilled labor," "climate as it affects operations," and "climate as an attraction to top management."

Plants in the 100-499 employee range also stressed "amicable labor relations" frequently. This factor and "ease of attracting out-of-state skilled labor, including research personnel," were both mentioned 32 times. As noted in Chapter V, many of the company officials treated amicable labor relations as equivalent to an absence of labor unions.

In the range of 25 to 99 employees, labor becomes somewhat less important, "Access to markets" was cited most often (73 times), "community facilities" next most frequently and "anticipated growth of markets" next in frequency.

Market access and expected growth of markets takes on overwhelming importance for small plants (0 to 24 employees), especially in developed counties. Similarly, low freight cost on shipping the final product is very often deemed an advantage by small plants.

Disadvantages Noted

The responding officials of the largest plants (500 or more employees) cited inadequacies of community facilities most often as disadvantages. Interviews disclosed that lack of facilities for the further education of research personnel was frequently regarded

TABLE 6.

All Factors Cited as Advantages in Florida by Size of Plant
1956 and 1957

Factor	0-24 employees	25-99 employees	100-499 employees	500 and more employees	Total
Access to markets	467	73	25	5	570
Anticipation of growth of markets	414	54	23	4	495
Amicable labor relations	218	21	32	6	277
Lower wages	170	39	18	5	232
Higher productivity	77	3	4	1	85
Florida labor laws	63	3	12	2	80
Availability of labor in Florida	270	43	30	5	348
Ease of attracting out-of-state skilled labor (including research personnel)	129	15	32	5	181
Low seller's mill price on raw materials and components	54	7	3	1	65
Low freight cost on obtaining raw materials and components	185	28	20	3	236
Availability of raw materials	151	24	14	4	193
Low cost of fuel	43	1	6	1	51
Low cost of electric power	77	1	4	1	83
Adequate supply and satisfactory type of water	51	6	12	4	73
Low cost of capital	8	2	0	0	10
Availability of capital	56	7	3	0	66
Low freight cost on shipping final product	295	40	22	1	358
Adequate waste disposal facilities	24	3	6	3	36
Climate (as it affects operations)	259	26	25	5	315
Community facilities (educational, medical, police and fire)	190	63	29	3	285
Community attitudes and aids	147	27	23	4	201
State and/or municipal tax structure	103	12	9	1	125
Climate (as an attraction to top management)	223	33	22	5	283
Personal (with economic advantages)	187	15	10	1	213
Personal (without economic advantages)	152	19	3	0	174
Aid from Florida Development Commission	22	0	1	0	23

TABLE 7.

Disadvantages Reported by Largest Plants (500 Employees and More)
(Number of times cited)

Factor	Original Plant	Branch Plant	Relocation of Out-of State Plant	Relocation of In-State Plant	Total
Freight cost on shipping final product	0	1	0	0	1
Community facilities (educational, medical, police, and fire)	0	2	1	0	3
Community attitudes and aid	0	1	0	0	1
State and/or municipal tax structure	0	0	1	0	1

TABLE 8.

Disadvantages Reported by Medium Size Plants (100-499 Employees)
(Number of times cited)

Factor	Original Plant	Branch Plant	Relocation of Out-of State Plant	Relocation of In-State Plant	Total
Productivity	0	1	0	0	1
Availability of labor already in Florida	0	2	0	0	2
Ease of attracting out-of-state skilled labor including research personnel)	0	0	1	1	2
Availability of raw materials	0	2	0	0	2
Cost of electric power	0	0	2	0	2
Availability of capital	0	0	1	0	1
Freight cost on shipping final product	0	0	1	0	1
Waste disposal possibilities	2	0	0	1	3
Climate (as it affects operation)	0	1	0	0	1
Community facilities (educational, medical, police, and fire)	1	5	3	0	9
Community attitudes and aid	0	1	0	0	1
State and/or municipal tax structure	3	1	1	0	5
Freight cost on obtaining raw materials and components	1	1	1	0	3

TABLE 9.

Disadvantages Reported by Rather Small Plants (25-99 Employees)
(Number of times cited)

Factor	Original Plant	Branch Plant	Relocation of In-State Plant	Relocation of Out-of State Plant	Total
Wages	10	0	1	0	11
Productivity	5	0	0	5	10
Ease of attracting out-of-state skilled labor (including research personnel)	0	0	2	0	2
Availability of raw materials	0	0	1	0	1
Cost of fuel	1	0	0	0	1
Cost of electric power	1	2	0	0	3
Supply and type of water	1	0	1	0	2
Availability of capital	11	0	0	0	11
Freight cost on shipping final product	0	10	1	0	11
Waste disposal possibilities	5	0	0	0	5
Community facilities (educational, medical, police, and fire)	1	0	2	6	9
State and/or municipal tax structure	1	0	0	5	6
Climate (an as attraction to top management)	0	1	0	0	1
Factors not listed	0	0	0	0	0
Freight cost on obtaining raw materials and components	1	1	0	0	2

as a significant drawback by managers of the largest plants. Plants in the 25 to 99 and 100 to 499 employee range also cited inadequate community facilities as a handicap. In the 25 to 99 employee range, availability of capital, freight cost on shipping final product, and wage rates were most often considered disadvantageous. The small plants—under 25 employees—on the other hand, considered difficulty of borrowing and high cost of electric power to be outstanding disadvantages. Small plants which relocated from out-of-state seem most often to have been impressed by the high cost of electric power in Florida, citing this condition more often as a disadvantage than any other factor. Tables 7 through 10 give a complete summary of disadvantages cited by respondents.

Summary Review

We have asserted that to be effective the state or local group interested in furthering industrial development must gain a thorough

TABLE 10.

Disadvantages Reported by Smallest Plants (1-24 Employees)
(Number of times cited)

Factor	Original Plant	Branch Plant	Relocation of Out-of State Plant	Relocation of In- State Plant	Total
Access to markets	25	10	0	0	35
Productivity	0	5	0	0	5
Availability of labor already in Florida	0	10	0	0	10
Ease of attracting out-of-state skilled labor (including research personnel)	15	0	0	0	15
Seller's mill price on raw materials and components	0	0	5	0	5
Availability of raw materials	0	1	5	0	6
Cost of fuel	0	0	1	0	1
Cost of electrical power	21	5	16	0	42
Availability of capital	35	0	10	0	45
Freight cost of shipping final product	16	21	1	0	38
Community facilities (educational, medical, poolice, and fire)	5	17	0	0	22
Community attitudes and aid	7	0	0	0	7
State and/or municipal tax structure	15	6	10	0	31
Freight cost on obtaining raw materials and components	13	10	6	5	34

grasp of the economies of its area. This entails a threefold stage of research. The one involves a survey of the kinds of industry located in the area and the reasons for their locations; the second delves into the types of industry which, if added on to those already there, would provide the area with an adequate industrial base; the third investigates particular industries to determine their price, cost, and hence location patterns so that ultimately the commission may determine which industries are the most likely prospects for its area.

This chapter has been concerned only with the first stage of research, the general location survey. More specifically, we have observed that a commission which has already determined which industries are in its area and what factors brought them there may analyze its data toward the end of determining how the underdeveloped counties may be expanded. As the same time it is important to ascertain which industry types tend to be attracted to developed counties, so that additional companies of these industry types can be encouraged to locate there. Most fundamentally, given a general industry type in an area (for example, the chemical industry), and given the knowledge of which factors induced its location there (for example, freight cost savings on raw materials), it is a simple step to the conjecture that chemical industry subtypes (for example, the paint, varnish and lacquer industry) may well have comparable location factors and that the subject area is already possessed of advantages which may well be vital to such industries. If the second stage study uncovers advantages in having a greater quantity of this industry type in the area (for example, if it would add necessary stability to the demand for labor in the area), a strong basis exists for going into research of the third stage, which oftentimes is the most expensive (and most rewarding) since it will be climaxed by an attempt to induce selected companies to locate in the subject area.

Need we observe finally at this point that if the research program has been well conducted, the quantity of information gained by the commission (when released to the prospect) will, to say the least, tend to encourage the prospect to locate in this area. Most likely, it is further the case that this same prospect was already considering the area as well as areas adjacent to it.[7]

---

[7]See M. L. Greenhut, "How to Explain the Recent Industrialization of the South," *Land Economics*, Nov., 1960., pp. 371-379.

CHAPTER VII

A POSTSCRIPT ON RECENT DEVELOPMENTS

The analysis of Florida locational factors contained in this book is based on a survey of new plants reported for 1956 and 1957. Since that time new industrial plants and major expansions have continued to add an average of nearly 25,000 jobs per year, according to Florida Development Commission data shown in Table 1.

TABLE 1.

Florida's New Industrial Plants: 1958-60

	1958	1959	1960
New Plants and Major Expansions	700	783	839
Expected Number of Employees	23,041	25,074	24,615

Source: *Florida's New Industrial Plants: 1960,* Business Research Report Number 122, Industrial Division, Florida Development Commission, Tallahassee.

A continued emphasis on relatively small plants is reflected in these data. Many of these plants were attracted by the rapid population growth in Dade County. The Florida Development Commission reported a total of 267 new plants in 1960 for Dade County, 237 of which were expected to employ less than 25 persons. Access to a rapidly growing market clearly continued to dominate these locational decisions. Forces on the demand side were probably largely responsible also for the continued rapid growth of new industrial employment in such counties as Orange, Broward, Duval, Palm Beach, Pinellas, and Hillsborough. In Brevard and Orange counties the missile testing facilities at Cape Canaveral have been of tremendous significance, and the recently announced "moon-shot" program for the area will insure further dramatic industrial expansion. Creation of additional facilities for consumer goods will go hand-in-hand with the erection of new electronics, engineering, research, and missile facilities. The highly technical nature of this prospective industrial development also points clearly to the vital importance of training and attracting "human capital"—knowledge and skills of educated people without whom complex material facilities can be useless.

Some caution in the use of data on the number of new industrial plants and the expected new employment which they

create is necessary if errors are to be avoided. First, no adjustment
is made for plants which go out of business. Since this occurs most
frequently in the case of small plants (due, for example, to the
owner's retirement or death), the effect on employment is smaller
than on the number of new facilities. Second, this factor may be
in part offset by the difficulty of securing information for very
small plants. Third, the employment shown is the number *expected*
to be employed within a reasonable period of time. Expectations
often change. Fourth, allocation of a plant to a particular year may
be arbitrary because the date of public announcement may be
quite different from date of commencement of construction. Fifth,
relocations of plants from one site in Florida to another may be
counted as new plants despite the attempt which is made to exclude
such facilities.

Changes in Population and Institutions

Florida's industrial growth and population growth were rapid
during the decade of the 1950's. Population increased from about
2.77 million in 1950 to about 4.95 million in 1960. The latter figure
brings the State into 10th place in the nation in this respect. This
compares with 31st place in 1930, 27th place in 1940, and 20th
place in 1950.[1] However, 13 of the State's 67 counties lost population between 1950 and 1960. These counties are all in North
Florida.[2] For the most part the population losses were heavy in
the young age group, particularly under 18 years, and generally
the loss of young people was higher among whites than among the
non-white population.[3]

It was noted in Chapter VI that small firms frequently cited
difficulty of securing needed financing and high cost of electric
power as disadvantages. The former would probably appear in a
survey of any state. The latter is due in part to a tendency of many

---

[1]*Statistics of Personal Income, Population, Construction, and Retail Trade
for Florida Counties,* Bureau of Economic and Business Research, University of
Florida, May, 1960, p. 17.

[2]Population losing counties are Calhoun, Gilchrist, Hamilton, Holmes, Jeffer-
son, Lafayette, Levy, Liberty, Madison, Suwannee, Union, Wakulla, and Wash-
ington.

[3]*Statistics of Personal Income, Population, Construction, Business and Manufacturing for Florida Counties,* Bureau of Economic and Business Research,
University of Florida, June, 1961, p. 18.

municipalities to use "profits" from the sale of electric power or natural gas as a substitute for property and other taxes. The effects of this system on plant location or expansion decisions are difficult to assess, but the practice is a shortsighted one if it keeps new plants in which electric power or gas is an important cost away from the community.[4]

Much change has taken place in the past few years in the institutional arrangements for financing the smaller firms. Under the Area Redevelopment Act federal loans and grants may be made in counties designated "redevelopment areas."[5] Federal financial assistance in the form of loans from the Small Business Administration is frequently directed toward rural areas. During the period July, 1959-May, 1960, this agency approved 541 loans totaling $30,144,000 for small businesses serving rural areas in the nation.[6] From the start of its lending operations in September, 1953, through December, 1960, the Small Business Administration approved 22,283 business loans for $1,051,453,000.[7] Both direct loans and loans in which banks participate are made by the agency. Participation loans make up more than three out of five loans. The extent of participation by Florida banks in this program appears to be increasing. In the first half of 1960 direct SBA loans in the State totaled about $2.2 million compared with about $0.8 million in participation loans. During the last half of the year direct loans of about $1.6 million were made compared with participation loans of about $1.3 million.[8]

The Small Business Administration is also active in licensing small business investment companies under authority of the Small Business Investment Act of 1958. As of September, 1961, a total of 354 such investment companies had been formed in the nation.[9] The Small Business Administration may lend a small business investment company up to $150,000 of the required starting capital

---

[4]For a discussion of some other implications of municipal "profits" from utilities, see M. R. Colberg, "Utility Profits: A Substitute for Property Taxes," *National Tax Journal*, Vol. VIII, No. 5, December, 1955.

[5]For an appraisal, see M. R. Colberg, "Area Relief: Will It Work?" *Industrial Development*, November, 1961.

[6]*Rural Development Program,* 5th Annual Report of the Secretary of Agriculture, September, 1960, p. 21.

[7]*15th Semiannual Report,* Small Business Administration, December 31, 1960.

[8]Computed from data in 15th *Semiannual Report* of SBA.

[9]"Rise of the SBIC's" *Wall Street Journal,* Sept. 9, 1961, p. 1.

of $300,000 through the purchase of subordinated debentures. The SBA can also lend operating funds to SBIC's. Recently there has been a trend toward larger loans through pooling of SBIC's resources, marking a trend away from the small loans for which the program was formed.[10]

Under Title V of the Small Business Investment Act of 1958 the agency is authorized to make loans to state and local development companies. (Florida has recently established a State Development Company.) The SBA may make loans in an amount equal to the development company's outstanding borrowings from all other sources. Development companies may purchase equity in, or make long-term loans to small firms. Small Business Administration loans of up to $250,000 for each small business may also be made to local development companies. More than 3000 local development companies have been established throughout the country.

The development since 1958 of new institutional arrangements for financing small firms has probably alleviated to a degree the problem of availability of capital frequently cited as a problem in the survey of new 1956 and 1957 plants in Florida. In general, SBA type of financial assistance, direct or indirect, to *any* small business—including firms in rural areas—appears to be preferable to the type available under the Area Redevelopment Act, where criteria for eligibility are necessarily arbitrary to a degree. In both cases, however, there is at least a partial substitution of funds derived from federal taxes for privately owned funds. This may constitute a dangerous trend in our economy, especially to the extent that federal funds *replace* private funds instead of entering marginal activities where private capital hesitates to go.

---

[10] *Ibid.*